UNCOVERING OUR HISTORY

Teaching with Primary Sources

SUSA

AMER
LIBRA
ASSOC
Chicago
2004

While extensive effort has gone into ensuring the reliability of information appearing in this book, the publisher makes no warranty, express or implied, on the accuracy or reliability of the information, and does not assume and hereby disclaims any liability to any person for any loss or damage caused by errors or omissions in this publication.

The paper used in this publication meets the minimum requirements of American National Standard for Information Sciences—Permanence of Paper for Printed Library Materials, ANSI Z39.48-1992. ∞

Library of Congress Cataloging-in-Publication Data

Veccia, Susan H.
    Uncovering our history : teaching with primary sources / Susan H. Veccia.
        p. cm.
    Includes bibliographical references and index.
    ISBN 0-8389-0862-4
    1. United States—History—Study and teaching.
    2. United States—History—Sources. 3. Library of Congress. National Digital Library Program.
    I. Title.
    E175.8.V43 2004
    973'.071—dc22   2003019893

Printed in the United States of America

08   07   06   05   04   5   4   3   2   1

CONTENTS

CHAPTER EIGHT

CHAPTER NINE

FOREWORD

When Susan Veccia asked me to write the foreword to this book, I immediately agreed to do so. Why? Two reasons stood out for me. First, I had worked with Susan on several projects focused on the Library of Congress's American Memory collections. Through that work I came to admire and respect Susan's work and to share her vision of American Memory as a resource without parallel for history teachers, school librarians, and students. The book she envisioned—this book—promised to make American Memory more accessible and useful to these audiences. Second, I knew all the other contributors either by working directly with them or by knowing indirectly about their work on other American Memory projects. Each contributor is an outstanding educator—whether a teacher or a librarian. Whether curriculum materials, ideas for teacher training, or conducting lessons with their own students, each person's work is always thoughtful and thought provoking. With these people as the authors, I thought, the book had to be a good one.

While I thought this would be a good book, after reading all the chapters I think this is not only a good book, it is a powerful one. Its power lies in the fact that each contributor provides us with significant snapshots of her or his personal journey to find ever-better ways to engage students directly with history. While the authors' successes are both heartening and instructive, each writer has also experienced her or his share of obstacles and pratfalls along the way. The strategies the writers have developed to cope with these problems empower the reader.

The stories are powerful in another sense. I discovered that the authors' professional journeys have, in fact, been in many ways similar to my own. Despite some obvious differences among us—geographical region, grade level, students, school settings, and resources—our journeys have led us over some common terrain (issues and problems) and in similar directions with respect to what works with students. As I read these stories, I was struck by how valuable a book like this one would have been to me as I stumbled along my own personal journey to become a better history teacher. Let me explain.

In the fall of 1967, because I was thinking about becoming a history teacher, I enrolled in a course titled "Social Foundations of Education," then the first required course in the teacher preparation program at the University of Colorado-Boulder. A few days into the course, Professor Jack Cousins sprang a test on the class. Our assignment was to answer as many of the fifty test questions as we could in twenty-five minutes. After the allotted time passed, Cousins began asking for volunteers to share their answers orally. About four or five questions in,

Cousins asked, "Okay, what was the name of the B-29 bomber that dropped the atomic bomb on Hiroshima in 1945?" My hand shot up immediately. Since I was the only student to raise my hand, Cousins called on me. "Enola Gay," I answered proudly. Cousins, of course, said, "Right!" Then, quite unexpectedly, he asked me, "So what?"

Having no ready answer, I was rather embarrassed by this question, which is no doubt why I still remember this episode so vividly. Cousins' deft handling of the situation allayed my brief public humiliation. An extraordinary teacher, Cousins used the sham test exercise to make several significant points about history teaching. One point—again burned indelibly into my memory—was that most history teachers spent far too much time covering the textbook and trans-mitting names and dates (what he called inert facts) to their students. Discrete facts, it seemed, had some inherent (although hidden) purpose and value. Further, teachers spent far too much time testing their students on their short-term reten-tion of those inert facts. (We soon found out that Jack had drawn the "test" items from commonly used textbooks and standardized tests.)

A second significant point was that this common approach to teaching history (i.e., coverage, textbooks, testing for facts) rested on certain assumptions about how students learn and what their actual involvement could be in the learning process. The most common assumption was that students needed the facts first, then they could think critically and historically about those facts. Unfortunately, in most history classrooms, teachers spent so much time imparting the facts that no time was left over to involve the students in thinking historically or critically about those facts.

A third point was that this approach to history teaching had further negative consequences. One was that students almost uniformly despised their history courses and they thought of them, by and large, as a waste of time. Because of this persistent attitude toward history courses, students had little motivation to learn and their performance on standardized history tests was dismal. (By the way, research suggests that little has changed in the last three-plus decades regard-ing these matters.)

Because Cousins was an exemplary teacher, he did not stop after making these important points. Rather, he involved the students in activities that illustrated more effective ways to engage students in their own learning. He drew many of the materials we used from the then current "new social studies" projects, most of which rested on a foundation of discipline-based inquiry. The learning activi-ties required students to uncover problems and issues, inquire into them, and find and use primary sources that informed critical inquiry into those problems.

Involved directly in the process of historical reconstruction, we discovered that the subjects were more interesting than we had thought before and we became more motivated to learn. We also discovered we were learning far more important skills and habits of mind than in the history courses we had had before. We discussed and argued about whether this or that source was more reliable, whether this or that had happened, and what warrants supported our thinking. What was more, we discovered we were gaining a better grasp of "conventional" historical facts because we had a purpose in learning them that we never had had before. So powerful were these experiences that I adopted an inquiry approach and the importance of "going to the source" as foundational elements of my emerging philosophy of what comprises effective history teaching.

It was not long before I had occasion to try to implement my emerging philosophy. I almost immediately discovered that there were all sorts of obstacles I had to negotiate if I were to engage my students in historical inquiry and primary sources. I will mention only three such obstacles, although there were many others. First, many students simply had difficulty reading and analyzing the sources. I discovered that my students were not as inherently interested as was I in many of the sources I brought to class. What to do? Although I didn't know the word at the time, I spent a good deal of time "scaffolding" the learning tasks and outcomes I expected students to do and achieve. I also found it was important to give students ownership of many of the problems, issues, and tasks they were to do. Such scaffolding increased both their interest and their abilities to deal with the sources in an intellectually respectable way. It also increased exponentially the time I had to devote to planning.

Second, I discovered that primary historical sources were not necessarily easy to come by or to make available to students. Imagine a time, not that long ago, when the Internet had not even been fancied a possibility! Imagine a time, too, when photocopying was only just beginning to appear on the scene. (How many of us still remember typing ditto masters if we wanted multiple copies of a page?) In this technological environment, I developed three strategies. One was to use "canned" source sets. These had one obvious advantage: a significant corpus of sources had already been culled from archives and libraries. A disadvantage was that my students did not always resonate to the topics. A second strategy was to "mine" every bookstore I entered for collections of primary documents. This approach, too, had its shortcomings: many of the sources in these books were irrelevant to the topics we wanted to study and I needed a wheelbarrow to carry all the books to class. My final strategy was to pester the research librarians I encountered. To a person, these folks were always willing and able to help. But again downsides: the primary materials to which they had access were often limited in scope and I still had to type the sources before I could use them with students.

Third, I discovered that some of my teaching assignments were not particularly conducive to engaging students with batches of primary sources. One of the first courses for which I had complete responsibility was a class of over three hundred students! The lecture hall I was assigned was the largest I had ever been in—and the seats were bolted to the floor. This was a survey course in United States history after 1865. Several "systemic" issues lurked below the surface of this course. One was that the department expected me to cover the entire sweep of U.S. history after the Civil War. A second expectation was that lecturing was the most efficient mode of transmitting information to students. A third was that three hundred students made it virtually impossible to use anything but objective tests over the material (who had time to read three hundred term papers or essay exams several times a semester?). A final obstacle was my own lack of imagination—I was both too new and too scared to think outside the box in which I found myself. It took time and experience to cope with these systemic problems.

In retrospect, I wish I had had a book like this one to help me get through some of the rough spots on my own personal journey. The craft wisdom that the contributors to this book bring to bear on the issue of effective history teaching is remarkable. Most important, the contributors to this book not only "talk the talk," they have "walked the walk." Through their personal stories, they share craft wisdom about how they have engaged their students directly with historical inquiry, primary sources, and technology. These stories provide the "real-classroom" test that all educators look for as they think about adopting new practices or refining others they may already use.

Second, our contributors' stories are powerful because they are honest and unvarnished. Each contributor suggests some of the pratfalls they took and the mistakes they made along the way. They candidly discuss many of the problems and obstacles they have encountered. They also describe for us the strategies they used to cope with these problems and obstacles. These strategies would have been helpful to me; they may be helpful to you as you embark on your own journey.

Finally, the themes that cut across these chapters resonate with my own experiences, with my own personal journey. What are some of these themes?

> Primary sources make history come alive for students when you involve them in authentic tasks.
>
> The constant interplay among big ideas (the "why" question; standards-based themes), nuts and bolts (the primary sources), and mediating skills (reading, source analysis) facilitates learning.
>
> Good questions are the engines of student inquiry. This has a corollary—to explore good questions in a satisfying way takes time.
>
> Since involving students with primary sources and questions will likely be new to most of them, and because of student diversity within most classrooms, students' experiences with these materials must be organized (scaffolded) carefully.
>
> Computer technology, although it can deliver incredible resources right into the classroom or library, has many pitfalls for which planning is a must.
>
> Collaboration, whatever the mix among teachers, librarians, and administrators, is a must if you are to succeed.
>
> Humility—don't assume you're going to get it "right" the first time; think of this effort as a journey and enjoy the lessons you learn along the way.

These themes emerge from the real classroom experiences of our contributors as they have tried to improve their own practice. Equally important, perhaps, is the fact that their experiences are consistent with the best current research in cognitive psychology, effective teaching, student motivation, integrating technology in instruction, and school change. This coming together of craft wisdom and solid research provides numerous warrants for believing that their advice to readers is sound.

James R. Giese
Hewit Institute for History and Social Science Education
University of Northern Colorado (Greeley)

CHAPTER ONE

Primary Sources:
Magical Moments
of Insight

I remember Miss Crivelli. She was a tall, buxom woman with clear creamy skin, bright red lipstick, and thick black hair piled high on her head. With a stentorian voice that bounced off the walls of the high school classroom, she would boom out questions and expect quick replies. She gazed theatrically beyond the front row to canvass the entire room. As a survival technique, I sat in the front row and hunkered down, hoping not to be noticed. I was a good student, but timid. I showed up on time and always did my homework. Homework consisted of memorizing mimeographed lists of names, historical events, and dates for the inevitable quiz the following day. Each night after dinner, I would retreat to my bedroom and memorize what I had to know. I excelled in the course but learned almost nothing about world history. Why? Apart from being scared stiff, nothing connected. Nothing was relevant to anything I knew or cared about. There were no "stories" in Miss Crivelli's classroom—only names, facts, and dates. And, certainly there were no primary sources! In fact, I didn't even know what primary sources were then . . . and I was a high school senior.

Fortunately, things have changed. Nearly every state in the nation requires the use of primary resources at some level in K–12 instruction. New York, for example, requires primary sources from kindergarten through twelfth grade. In Virginia, primary sources are introduced in the fourth grade. Sometimes these requirements surface in state history or social studies frameworks; sometimes in the library and information literacy competencies. Sometimes both. Increasingly, teachers are obliged to teach to these standards across the curriculum.

Primary sources by themselves seem dull and boring. Why, then, should they be *required* in K–12 instruction? In the hands of a creative teacher, primary sources add a human backdrop to the study of history and extend the focus from what happened to its meaning—what it meant then, what it means now, and what it might mean in the future. When used creatively, primary sources can personalize the learning process, helping students to understand their own history and connect it to larger issues.

Primary sources can provide the framework for spirited classroom discussions, debates, and projects that will engage students in memorable ways. Primary sources inevitably evoke more questions than answers. Think for a minute about Miss Crivelli's classroom. Where were the questions? The memorization she demanded required only answers and provided no relevance to my life. Powered by mindless repetition, it skipped the "story" in history, the colorful threads that weave many shapes and textures of experiences into an expressive, memorable whole. The classroom was focused on the teacher. Miss Crivelli very effectively taught a number of important skills—reading, organization, test taking—but she did not teach history. I wonder what she would have done if she had had access to the wealth of primary-source materials available to teachers today. Would her teaching techniques have changed?

FINDING AND UNDERSTANDING PRIMARY SOURCES

The requirement to use primary sources poses a dilemma for many educators. While required to use primary sources, until the mid-1990s it was difficult to find appropriate primary sources. Those teachers who wanted to use primary sources would dig into their personal materials or buy individual replicas for use in the classroom. Without easy access to appropriate materials, many other teachers just didn't use primary sources in their classrooms at all.

How do teachers who now have unprecedented access to primary sources know the "good" from the "bad," having had little firsthand experience? How do they recognize what viewpoints are represented? How do they identify primary sources that fit curriculum objectives? Having never used primary sources, how do teachers know what to do with them? It is not like picking up a textbook or teaching a ready-made curriculum. Primary sources are different. Unlike working with many other teaching resources, using primary sources requires significant research and critical-thinking skills.

Before teachers can effectively use primary sources, they must understand the nature of primary sources, which is often not taught in teacher education or library schools. In recent years, a few books have been published that have helped educators—both teachers and library media specialists—better understand primary sources. Of particular note is the September/October 2000 issue of the American Association of School Librarians (AASL) professional journal *Knowledge Quest*. The entire issue is devoted to primary sources and should be on every teacher's professional reading shelf. It provides short articles written by teachers and school library media specialists.

Through the voices of educators who have effectively used primary sources, *Uncovering Our History* provides a practical introduction to the value of these materials in elementary and secondary education. It provides sample activities and lesson plans for elementary, middle school and high school teachers, and school media specialists. It will be useful for professional development as well. It provides frameworks for conducting workshops on the nature of primary sources from the Library of Congress online collections and how to use them in K–12 education.

WHAT ARE PRIMARY SOURCES?

Primary sources are manuscripts, first-person diaries, oral histories, letters, interviews, photographs, maps, films, sound recordings, music, song sheets—fragments of history, incomplete in themselves, but when assembled, analyzed, and researched, they can provide personal insights, human drama, and deep historical understandings. Primary sources can also be places and people. They are resources that speak directly to the viewer, the reader, and the listener without explanatory context. They evoke a sense of time and place. They often carry a point of view and thus, by definition, are not always neutral or objective. This means that one primary source can contradict another—or corroborate another. Educators must understand how to work with these ambiguities and help students construct the context for deeper understandings. This can be done even with very young children.

Personal Stories

When you think about the personal nature of primary sources, you begin to understand their power to unleash fascinating stories that will engage student interest. For example, the Vietnam Memorial is one of the most frequented tourist destinations in Washington, D.C. The massive black marble wall slopes deeper and deeper into the ground, symbolizing the nation's becoming more involved in the war. The wall is unadorned except for the names of American servicemen and women killed in action, year by year. The names are engraved in simple and uniform lettering on each successive panel as the years progressed. Visiting the wall and observing friends and family who gather by the wall to trace their loved one's name from the wall or to leave personal tokens behind personalize history in hundreds, if not thousands, of poignant ways. Those items left at the wall are collected at the end of each day and held at the Smithsonian Institution. Think about how visiting the wall or examining some of the primary sources left at the wall—letters, poems, photographs—could inform today's students who are trying to understand the heart-felt, tragic issues that my generation remembers about Vietnam. This is part of my history; perhaps it is a part of yours as well. But it is not part of our students' remembered history. Primary sources can tell so many stories from so many human perspectives. Taken together, they provide a different kind of experience and understanding from what can be acquired from reading a textbook.

Until recently, many educators' concept of primary sources had been limited to historical documents such as the Declaration of Independence or the U.S. Constitution, both of which can be found in textbooks. While documents such as these are important in the understanding of American history, the printed texts of these documents are not necessarily the kind of materials that excite students. Consider instead a handwritten text—an electronic replica of the "first draft" of the Declaration of Independence, with tatters, tears, and marginalia in Jefferson's hand.

This document shown (see figure 1-1) is found on the Library of Congress website and raises many interesting questions.[1] The document was written by Thomas Jefferson, John Adams, and Benjamin Franklin; others amended it. What does this tell us about democracy and the art of compromise? Are there any parallels in today's government? What does this facsimile tell us about the differences between Jefferson, and, for example, John Adams? How would you research this further? What can the document tell us about the writing process? About collaborative writing theory?

How would you modify this type of lesson to interest younger children? Ask Monica Edinger, a fourth-grade teacher at Dalton School. Monica worked not with the Declaration of Independence, but with the Constitution. She asked her elementary school students to annotate the Constitution, building a glossary of unfamiliar words, historical images, and background information that would be helpful in answering other children's questions.[2] "What does tranquility mean, Ms. Edinger?" her students inquire.

Once you start using primary sources with students, one of the things you will discover is that the students will soon have more questions. Many questions! While primary sources can be used to illustrate a point, the questions they raise are possibly more important. Sometimes you don't have enough information from the primary source to answer the specific question you are researching. But, the item may stimulate many more questions that *can* be researched. Often the value of the primary document, the term "document" used here in the broadest sense, depends upon the questions that it generates and the resulting inquiries.

Ongoing Investigations

Apart from the fact that primary sources are required by most states, teachers who use primary sources report that students begin to think like historians and enjoy the discovery process. They look at history as ongoing investigations that they are directing. They learn to consider many different kinds of sources, not just books, but diaries and interviews of family members who may have experienced an important historical event. Listen to this high school student in Missouri interviewing her grandmother about World War II:

> As I conducted this interview, I learned a great deal about the war. Much of what we learn in school is about memorable battles and special dates. What I learned from my Grandma is that a lot changed on the home front during the war, more than what is documented in history books. She experienced the war through the eyes of a nine-year-old child. It is not likely to be something that she forgets nor is this interview.

Primary sources provide human interest—the incentive for students to want to learn more. If students are to appreciate the significance of these personal stories, prior knowledge is often required. For example, students may or may not know that Walt Whitman was a nurse during the Civil War and that he visited the wounded in a barn, which had been converted into a field hospital. Armed with this knowledge, however, when students find an image of that barn *and* handwritten notes of Whitman's hospital visits in the Library of Congress online

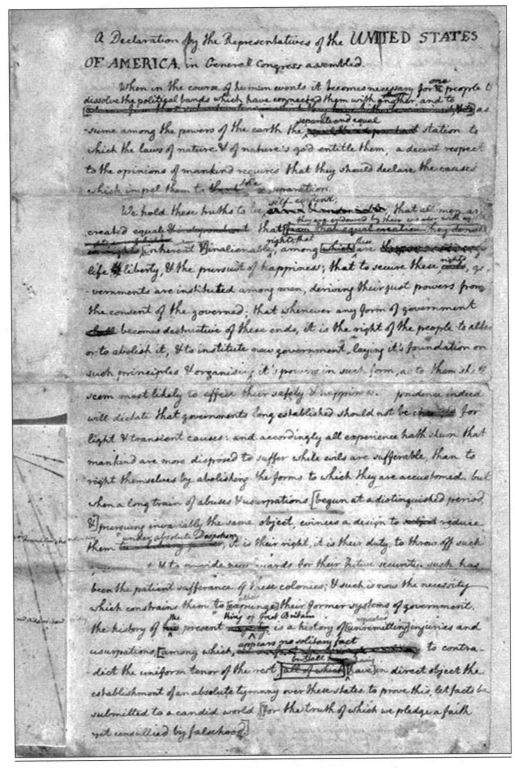

Figure 1-1
The "first draft" of the Declaration of Independence shows marginalia in Jefferson's hand. From the online exhibition *American Treasures of the Library of Congress*.

collections they will no doubt experience a sense of "Wow!" The immediacy of first-person written or spoken accounts coupled with a visual image of "place" is compelling to many students. One teacher noted, "In sharing the Whitman hospital [notebooks], I clearly saw a sheen of tears in students' eyes and noted an avid interest in Civil War soldiers as 'people,' not simply as pallid historical figures."

On a basic level, developing chronological skills is an important part of understanding history, which can be enhanced by using primary sources. One Michigan student commented, "I learned that in order to do history, one must be objective and be able to look at a puzzle of historical events and put them in order." Seeing themselves in this chronological, historical continuum helps children understand that we all participate in the making of history—every day—and that each of us in the course of our lives leaves behind materials that could become part of the "historical record." When students grasp this, they better understand the nature of primary sources—their strengths and their limitations.

Look at the "Mindwalk Activity" on the Library of Congress website for an excellent exercise to use with teachers and students first learning about primary sources.[3] Designed by James Giese, then director of the National Consortium for Social Studies Education, this activity asks students to reconstruct their day, listing what items might be found as evidence of their daily life—things like telephone or e-mail messages, diary entries, photographs, calendars, school records, etc. This activity walks students through a close observation and evaluation process by which they will come to understand that the historical record is both vast *and* limited because of the sometimes ephemeral and personal nature of primary sources.

As everyday evidence of life, primary sources can provide a glimpse into popular culture. Consider, for example, this early twentieth-century baseball card (see figures 1-2 and 1-3). Distributed in cigarette packs, these baseball cards were the forerunners to modern trading cards.

On another level, to make sense of primary sources, students learn to think more critically—to be observant and objective before they can draw inferences from an item or a set of items. One inference that can be drawn is point of view. What is the intent of the speaker, the photographer, the writer? How do you interpret this point of view within the time period? Working with primary sources is not always neat and tidy. In fact, it is often quite messy. Listen to this student's observation:

> Simple topics have a tendency to head toward complicated quickly. Something that seems crystal clear always becomes hazy; especially when primary sources contradict themselves. As a historian, you can never let yourself be absorbed by one thing.

This student has learned something very important that is not always recognized even by today's professional news media. Important issues have many points of view that must be considered for true understanding.

Consider, for example, this Timothy O'Sullivan photograph of the Gettysburg battlefield in the Matthew Brady Civil War collection from the Library of Congress. O'Sullivan was one of Matthew Brady's field photographers whose job was to accompany the Union troops and document life on the battlefield. In a well-documented and researched case, this O'Sullivan photograph of the dead in

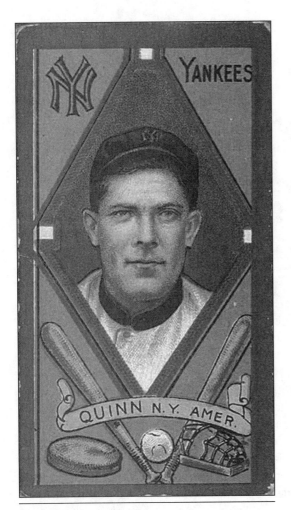

Figure 1-2
This early twentieth-century baseball card of "Jack" Quinn provides evidence of popular culture.

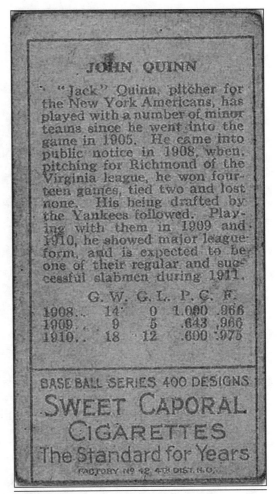

Figure 1-3
Verso of "Jack" Quinn baseball card.

Gettysburg was used by Alexander Gardner, a colleague and competitor of Brady's, to suggest atrocities by *both* the Union and the Confederate sides (see figure 1-4). While a photograph records an authentic image, what the photographer chooses to capture can be used to convey different messages.[4]

Raw and Unvarnished Materials

In addition to primary sources being messy, ambiguous, and sometimes contradictory, because they present themselves as seen through their creator's eyes, they are raw and unvarnished. If it is text, the language could be difficult to understand or considered rough and offensive in today's world. Likewise, visuals could be unsettling to some students, depending upon their backgrounds. Primary sources, thus,

Figure 1-4
"Does the Photographer Lie?" This Timothy O'Sullivan photograph is found in *Selected Civil War Photographs, 1861–1865,* American Memory collection.

require teachers to introduce them within the historical context of time. Things were different then. Materials emotionally difficult for today's students are a part of the historical record and can be used to help students think more critically about the past. In this day of sensitivity to Internet content and filtering of websites in schools around the country, this is, I think, an important issue to address up front. For some firsthand advice, consult Frances Jacobson's excellent article in *Knowledge Quest,* "The Dark Side of Primary Sources."[5] Teachers need to know that primary sources do not come with a *Good Housekeeping* seal of approval. This is not necessarily a bad thing, but it requires teacher and student preparation.

ACCESS TO PRIMARY SOURCE COLLECTIONS

Using primary resources leads into an almost endless research journey. The breadth of primary source materials is unlimited. How do teachers and students find appropriate materials? *Where* do they look? *How* do they look? How do they evaluate what they have found? Enter the school library media specialist.

A Team Approach: Teachers and School Librarian

Incorporating primary sources into the curriculum provides the ideal opportunity for library media specialists to work more closely with *all* teachers, particularly history and social studies teachers. Librarians trained in research methods can short-circuit some of the frustrations many teachers associate with finding appropriate resources online. (Chapter 3 addresses the intricacies of online searching in considerable detail.) For the librarian, this is an ideal working environment for enriching the school library collection—both physical and virtual—and to ensure that the collection remains relevant and grows with the needs of the students and teachers. It is also a wonderful opportunity to build stronger information-literacy skills among teachers and students alike. A team approach will strengthen the curriculum and build a more vibrant library media program. This is collaborative learning in its truest sense.

Virtual Library Collections

Collections that house rich primary sources are held by federal and university libraries, historical societies, archives, and private collections often far beyond the reach of most school teachers and librarians. The Web, however, has provided many of these institutions—and even individuals—the means to share their hitherto "hidden" materials with the world at large. There are now dozens of reputable Internet sites, both public and private, that provide access to primary-source collections, in some cases with specialized teaching tools.

FEDERAL GOVERNMENT DIGITAL RESOURCES

The National Archives and Records Administration holds official government records. This includes such things as the founding national documents (the Declaration of Independence, the Constitution, the Bill of Rights); the official records of the standing, special, select, and joint committees of the House of Representatives and the Senate; federal court records; census records; military records; ship-passenger arrival records; passport records, and the like. In addition to text, there are materials in a variety of formats, including maps, motion pictures, photographs, and graphic works. The volume of these records is exhaustive. A small percentage of these records are online in the National Archives Archival Information Locator, known informally as NAIL. The Archives provide teacher training and materials through its Digital Classroom.

The National Park Service sponsors *Links to the Past,* a website that provides a series of educational exhibits about Park Service historical sites. Organized into four sections—People, Places, Objects, and Events—educational materials, many of which are primary sources, are available for further study. Here you will find, for example, selected Revolutionary War artifacts from Park Service museums. Its educational outreach program, *Teaching with Historical Places,* offers online lesson plans based on properties listed in the National Register.

PRIVATE SECTOR DIGITAL RESOURCES

From the private sector there is *HarpWeek,* a professionally indexed full-text website of *Harper's Weekly,* 1857–1912. This time frame covers the Civil War, Reconstruction, and the Gilded Age. *Harper's* was an influential publication in its day, publishing editorial comment along with illustrations and cartoons by Winslow Homer and Thomas Nast. While its subscription rate may well be beyond the reach of school libraries, this site now provides ten online exhibits, each of which contains a wealth of primary-source materials. It is well worth visiting.

Selected Primary-Source Collections

The National Archives and Records Administration

(http://www.archives.gov/index.html)

The Archives contains the official records of government. Here you will find federal court records; census records; military records; ship-passenger arrival records; and passport records. A small percentage of these materials are available online. The Digital Classroom provides context for K–12 teachers.

The National Park Service

(http://www.cr.nps.gov/history/)

Links to the Past is a series of educational exhibits about National Park Service (NPS) historical sites. Here you will find artifacts from NPS museums as well as lesson plans relating to historical sites.

HarpWeek

(http://www.harpweek.com/)

This professionally indexed full-text site of *Harper's Weekly* is available by subscription, but it provides publicly available thematic exhibits based on primary-source materials, 1857–1912.

History Matters

(http://historymatters.gmu.edu/)

This collaborative site provides annotated selections of primary sources about ordinary Americans as well as lesson plans and an impressive gateway to other online sources.

The California Heritage Collection

(http://sunsite.berkeley.edu/CalHeritage/)

This collection from Berkeley highlights the history of California and the opening of the American West.

Douglass Archives of American Public Address

(http://douglass.speech.nwu.edu/)

This collection of speeches from Northwestern University is assembled for the study of rhetoric. Many of these speeches have not been previously anthologized.

Duke University, Rare Book, Manuscript, and Special Collections Library

(http://scriptorium.lib.duke.edu/)

Duke University has made many of its special collections available on the Web including Civil War commentary by women, a collection on nineteenth-century advertising, and a collection of nineteenth-century songsheets.

The Valley of the Shadow Project

(http://www.iath.virginia.edu/vshadow2/choosepart.html)

This project from the University of Virginia tells the story of two communities—one in the North and one in the South—during the Civil War.

Documenting the American South

(http://docsouth.unc.edu/dasmain.html)

This site from the University of North Carolina at Chapel Hill is a collection of resources about the South, including slave narratives.

The American Memory Historical Collections

(www.loc.gov/)

The National Digital Library of the Library of Congress has more than 100 collections of primary sources related to the history and culture of America. Guidance, including online lesson plans, feature presentations, and student activities, is provided through the Learning Page.

RESEARCH LIBRARY DIGITAL RESOURCES

Increasingly, universities and scholars are sharing their existing collections via the Web and, in some cases, building special collections for the Web. The *Valley of the Shadow* project from the University of Virginia provides thousands of Civil War artifacts from two communities, one Northern and one Southern. Materials include newspaper accounts, diaries, letters, maps, church records, and military records. Included as well are online lesson plans designed for secondary school teachers.

History Matters, a joint project of the American Social History Project at the City University of New York and the Center for History and New Media at

George Mason University, is a website designed for high school and college teachers. It provides over 700 selected primary-source documents about the experiences of ordinary Americans throughout U.S. history. All materials have been vetted by historians and are annotated to address their larger historical significance and context. This site also provides an excellent gateway to lesson plans and other digital primary and secondary source collections with independent site reviews from the *Journal of American History*.

The University of California at Berkeley has the *California Heritage Collection*, an online collection of more than 30,000 items relating to California's history. Northwestern University provides the *Douglass Archives of American Public Address*, an online collection of speeches for rhetorical study. Duke University's Rare Book, Manuscript, and Special Collections Library provides more than a dozen primary source collections and exhibits including *Civil War Women*, a website focusing on three nineteenth-century women and their stories. Two other Duke online collections, *Emergence of Advertising in America, 1850–1920* and *Historic Sheet Music*, are noteworthy not only because of their content but because they were developed in conjunction with the Library of Congress. The same is true of *Documenting the American South*, a collection of sources from the University of North Carolina at Chapel Hill on Southern history, literature, and culture from the colonial period through the first decades of the twentieth century. These collaborations are discussed more fully in chapter 2.

These are but a few examples of the wealth of primary source materials available, mostly for free, on the Internet.

The American Memory Historical Collections

Uncovering Our History addresses the Library of Congress American Memory Historical Collections—over 7.5 million primary sources that are freely available from the Library of Congress website—and how to make effective use of them in K–12 instruction. The American Memory project was an innovative effort by the National Digital Library Program of the Library of Congress to digitize the library's Americana special collections and to facilitate the digitization of other significant research collections nationwide. These materials can be found on the Library of Congress website. The National Digital Library Program, the American Memory Historical Collections, and the American Memory Fellows Program are discussed in chapter 2.

INFORMATION LITERACY AND CRITICAL THINKING

Working effectively with American Memory primary-source materials in K–12 education requires a different way of thinking from what most of us experienced in our own elementary and secondary education. It requires educators to help students think more critically about what they are reading, viewing, or hearing. It requires students to differentiate between objective and subjective interpretations and to understand what more they need to know before they can make reasonable conclusions. This is a sophisticated process.

Using primary sources with K–12 students requires understanding these ambiguities, developing research and critical-thinking skills, and designing lesson plans around primary source materials. Librarians will immediately see a heavy dose of information-literacy skills embedded in this process. Teachers will see endless opportunities to engage their students in creative ways. When primary sources are integrated into the curriculum in this fashion, magical moments of student insight can occur, as you will hear in the voices of the contributing authors of this book.

CURRICULUM INTEGRATION AND PROFESSIONAL DEVELOPMENT

This book, a collaborative effort among colleagues who have used American Memory resources with their own students in classrooms and libraries across the nation, is intended to help the reader better understand the nature of primary resources and how powerful they can be in education. Focused on the digital resources from the Library of Congress, and specifically on the American Memory collections, it is planned both as a conceptual and practical guide to understanding and using primary sources in K–12 instruction.

Primary sources can't just be "tacked on" to an existing curriculum; they must be seamlessly integrated into the curriculum. The important topic of developing curriculum connections with primary sources is explored in some detail in chapter 4 by Stanlee Brimberg, a teacher at Bank Street School for Children in New York City and a longtime Library of Congress workshop facilitator.

Curriculum connections with primary sources can happen on all levels of K–12 instruction. Nothing communicates better than personal experience. Gail Petri, librarian at Fyle Elementary School in Rochester, New York, discusses her experiences with elementary school students in chapter 5. Laura Wakefield, teacher at Neptune Middle School in Kissimmee, Florida, relates her middle school experience in chapter 6. And, Michael Federspiel, coordinator of social studies for the Midland Public Schools in Michigan, writes in chapter 7 about using primary sources with high school students. Gail, Laura, and Mike are active American Memory Fellows and have extensive experience working with Library of Congress online materials.

Chapters 8 and 9 address professional development. Chapter 8 provides a framework for designing your own workshop using materials and services of the Library of Congress. Model workshops are suggested with links to online lesson plans, templates, and other tools for educators. Chapter 9 provides an inspirational map for this journey of discovery and learning.

EXPANDING ROLE OF THE LIBRARY MEDIA SPECIALIST

The research domain of the school librarian has expanded exponentially, and with this growth, part of the dilemma of primary sources has been solved. There is now an abundance of primary sources available electronically. With unprecedented access to primary sources through the Internet, educators now have access to a wealth of materials that can enrich their understanding of primary sources in teaching and learning. What to do with them remains the critical question that this book begins to address.

NOTES

1. First draft of the Declaration of Independence, *American Treasures of the Library of Congress* [online], available from http://www.loc.gov/exhibits/treasures/tr00.html.

2. Monica Edinger, *Seeking History: Teaching with Primary Sources in Grades 4–6* (Portsmouth, N.H.: Heinemann, 2000).

3. Mindwalk Activity. Historian's Sources. The Learning Page. American Memory Historical Collections [online], available from http://memory.loc.gov/ammem/ndlpedu/lessons/psources/mindwalk.html.

4. "Does the Camera Ever Lie?" *Selected Civil War Photographs, 1861–1865*, American Memory Collection [online], available from http://memory.loc.gov/ammem/cwphtml/cwpcam/cwcam1.html

5. Frances F. Jacobson, "The Dark Side of Primary Sources," *Knowledge Quest* 29, no. 1 (September/October 2000): 35–37.

CHAPTER TWO

The American Memory Website from the Library of Congress

It's a library without walls—an electronic archive of primary source materials. It's an online destination for schoolchildren, visiting side-by-side with scholars. It provides resources for lifelong learning at all levels, for all people, open twenty-four hours a day, seven days a week. It is a tool for research, enabling a myriad of access points beyond traditional author-title-subject cataloging information. It's an integrated platform for accessing multiple media formats—the written word, the spoken word—as seen or heard in manuscripts, books, films, music, maps, letters, diaries, interviews, speeches, photographs, drawings, pamphlets, posters, cartoons, song sheets, sheet music, and more. It's a catalyst for library digitization nationwide. It is a distributed network of electronic resources shared among libraries. The American Memory Historical Collections, which can be accessed from the Library of Congress's home page (see figure 2-1), are all of these things.

The American Memory website provides free access to over 100 primary source collections and more than 7.5 million items from the Library of Congress, the world's largest research library. These materials can expand the collections of school and public libraries exponentially. This chapter briefly summarizes the library's digital offerings, focusing largely on American Memory and its online collections of particular interest to K–12 educators.

INFORMATION DEMOCRACY

Free and equal access to information is at the heart of the American library system. By making the contents of the Library of Congress's specialized collections freely available online, the library's historical and cultural resources can be

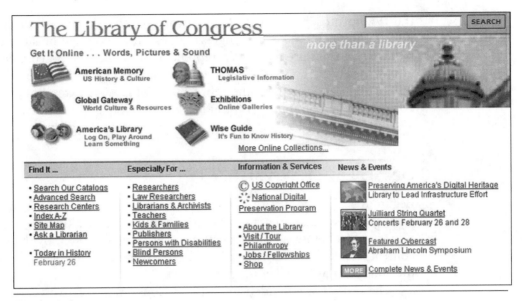

Figure 2-1
The American Memory Historical Collections are found on the
Library of Congress website, http://www.loc.gov.

widely shared. While the library's catalog has been online internally and available
to members of Congress since 1980, it wasn't until 1992 that the catalog became
accessible to external researchers via Telnet; in 1993 it became publicly accessible
on the Web.

However, as important as catalog information is to researchers, it does not
provide an electronic facsimile of the item itself. After identifying an item in the
online catalog, in most cases a researcher still needs to come to the Library of
Congress in Washington, D.C., to obtain the item—be it a book, a photograph,
or a sound recording. It is only through digitizing each item—by scanning each
item and converting the text, image, or sound to an electronic format—that a cataloged library item becomes truly "accessible" to the public. In the early 1990s,
when the Library of Congress was piloting this project, James H. Billington,
Librarian of Congress, spoke of this process as "getting the champagne out of the
bottle." By 1995, the digitization of the American Memory collections was well
under way, and the champagne was beginning to flow at the National Digital
Library, which is discussed later in this chapter. That same year, THOMAS, the
Library of Congress legislative tracking system, previously only available internally and to Congress, went on the Web for public access.

Today, the Web and digital technology are pervasive. Billington often refers to
the effect of the World Wide Web as the twentieth-century equivalent to the
opening up of nineteenth-century public reading rooms. In the library world, it
has fundamentally changed information presentation and distribution. This trans-
formation of libraries has facilitated "information democracy," a phrase once
used to describe American Memory by a university librarian who participated in

the 1990 prototype. By making its historical and cultural collections freely available to all, the Library of Congress hopes "to encourage broad and full participation in citizenship and the entrepreneurship which free, dynamic and self-governing societies require."[1] This is no modest goal. No longer the exclusive domain of Congress and scholars, the Library of Congress is extending its reach to new constituencies beginning with the K–12 educational community.

THE NATIONAL DIGITAL LIBRARY

Begun in 1995, the National Digital Library was established as a public-private partnership to plan the massive $60-million undertaking to convert selected Library of Congress special collections to electronic content by the year 2000. The content is called the American Memory Historical Collections. Figure 2-2 shows the American Memory home page.

The project was funded initially by Congress for a five-year period, and for every appropriated dollar, the library raised three private dollars from foundations and charitable individuals. John W. Kluge and the David and Lucile Packard Foundation each gave $5 million right from the start. Many other foundations

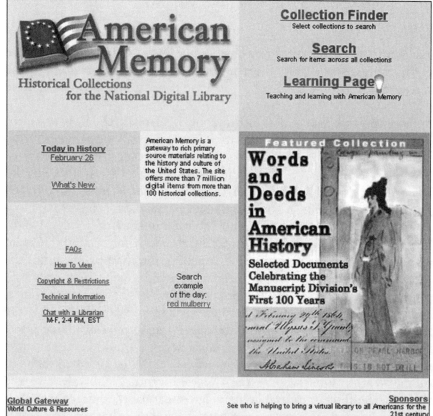

Figure 2-2
The American Memory website (http://www.memory.loc) provides free access to millions of primary source documents.

and individuals gave considerable resources and participated in significant ways. These generous donors are officially recognized on the Library of Congress website.

The National Digital Library met its five-year goal of converting 5 million digital items by 2000, the year of the Library of Congress's bicentennial celebration. On its two-hundredth birthday, Billington proudly presented the American Memory collections as "A Gift to the Nation." Today, the Library of Congress online collections exceed 7.5 million digital items. Since 2001, the digitization program of the library's special collections has been integrated into its day-to-day operations.

Collaborations

As the Library of Congress digital program was moving forward, so, too, was an effort to develop technical standards for digitization of library collections. In 1995, the Library of Congress joined with the Council on Library and Information Resources (CLIR), fourteen research libraries, and the National Archives and Records Administration (NARA) to form the Digital Library Federation for the purpose of sharing ideas on building a digital repository and developing interoperability standards.

As a demonstration of interoperability, through a 1997 gift from Ameritech, the Library of Congress sponsored a three-year competition that funded the digitization of thirty-three library collections from libraries across the nation. Some of these collections, while searchable through the American Memory website, actually reside on other institutional servers, thus forming the beginning of a distributed network of primary-source materials. Taken as a whole, these collections provide regional focus of national significance. As an example, *Small-Town America, 1850–1920* is a delightful stereoscopic collection from the New York Public Library depicting everyday life in towns, villages, and cities in the Northeast. The *African-American Experience in Ohio* is a multi-format collection of manuscripts, texts, and images relating to black history in Ohio, 1850–1920. These collections complement the holdings of the Library of Congress. Largely, the American Memory collections represent the strengths of the Library of Congress and its wide array of collections on American history and culture. Many of these collections are described later in this chapter, and figures 2-3 through 2-6 show some of the types of collections that are included.

A Learning Place

As a historian who is deeply concerned about the state of education in this country, Librarian of Congress James Billington did not envision a static online resource but rather one that would become a catalyst to education and lifelong learning. He envisioned a place populated by humanistic materials of all sorts that would stimulate questions and further research, a place where memories can be preserved, collected, and savored by future generations. He envisioned a place for learning, not necessarily a place "to find information." This would not happen without human mediators, he concluded.

Figure 2-3
The Alexander Graham Bell Family Papers is an example
of a privately funded archival collection held at the Library of Congress.

Figure 2-4
The Hannah Arendt Papers is an American Memory collection that
required special treatment for its copyrighted materials.

Figure 2-5
The African-American Experience in Ohio is an Ameritech-funded collaborative
American Memory project with the Ohio Historical Society.

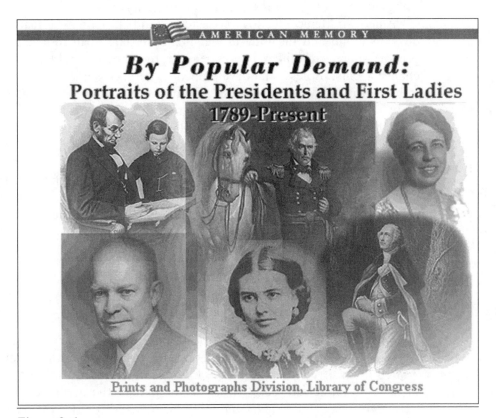

Figure 2-6
By Popular Demand: Portraits of the Presidents and First Ladies is an example of
a frequently requested series of photographs.

THE AMERICAN MEMORY FELLOWS PROGRAM

Thus, as a part of the five-year plan, an aggressive outreach program for teachers and school library media specialists was inaugurated. This was called the American Memory Fellows Program, a five-year program (1997–2001) through which Library of Congress staff worked with teams of K–12 teachers and librarians across the country to help them understand the nature of primary sources and incorporate them into their everyday curricula. This ambitious project was undertaken with guidance from the Center for Children and Technology (CCT) in New York. Through the work of Bill Tally, a senior CCT researcher, and other educational colleagues, the library became acquainted with best practices of teaching and learning.

Library staff worked closely with creative teachers and school library media specialists to build a practical, hands-on program for educators wishing to use Library of Congress primary sources in their classrooms and libraries. A strong emphasis was placed on partnerships between school library media specialists and teachers for developing teaching materials. Because the Library of Congress needed to get this program up and running fast, it sought educators who already had some technology skills and who also had reliable Web access at school. Technology skills were never critical instructional components; yet many fellows reported that they had become more technically proficient and more confident using the technology by the conclusion of the program.

American Memory Fellows were to be trailblazers: master teachers who could develop sound and meaningful teaching materials to introduce the concepts of primary sources to others. Fundamentally, the library sought educational leaders, change agents, professional development experts—people who could work hand-in-hand with library staff to extend Library of Congress digital resources into many different types of schools across the country.

While the American Memory Fellows Program has now concluded, the Learning Page (http://memory.loc.gov/learn/), designed initially for that program, continues to support all K–12 educators who use Library of Congress primary-source collections. The legacy of the Fellows program lives on in teacher-developed lessons designed in the course of the five years. In addition, many of the workshops designed for that program are now available on the Learning Page. The Learning Page is discussed more fully in chapter 3, and frameworks for using existing professional-development materials are discussed in chapter 8.

THE LIBRARY OF CONGRESS COLLECTIONS

Measured by its collections, the Library of Congress is the biggest library in the world. It houses more than 120 million items on 530 *miles* of shelving! More than 33,000 items arrive daily from the library's various acquisitions programs, and, of these items, about 10,000 will become part of the permanent collection. The library collects in all formats and in 460 languages. It holds the papers of twenty-three presidents. In addition to books and manuscripts, it has music, map, recorded sound, photographs, motion pictures, ethnographic, newspaper, and comic book collections, and more. Established in 1800 by an act of Congress, the

Library of Congress and its collections continue to reflect the philosophy of its founding father, Thomas Jefferson, who once said, there was "no subject to which a Member of Congress may not have occasion to refer."[2] Yet, this does not mean library materials are acquired indiscriminately. While a copy of every item copyrighted must be deposited at the Library of Congress, contrary to popular notion, the library does *not* automatically include each copyright deposit in its permanent collection.

Clearly, these massive collections cannot all be digitized for online presentation in American Memory. How does the library decide what to convert to online content?

Selection of Online Content

Just as book selection is critical to building a useful school library, so, too, are digitization decisions important for building a national digital library. Given the scope of the Library of Congress collections, hard choices must be made. It is often erroneously thought that "the content" of the Library of Congress is being converted to digital format. Not only would this be an extremely costly endeavor, but given its massive collections, the freight train fully loaded would never come into the station.

FULL COLLECTIONS OR INDIVIDUAL ITEMS?

Will it be piece-by-piece conversion, or collection-by-collection conversion? Most libraries strive to develop "comprehensive" collections to support the research or information needs of its primary users. Usually school libraries do this by acquiring individual items. University and national libraries also acquire collections of items as well as individual items. Thus, for the most part, the Library of Congress American Memory project began by selecting full archival collections—not individual items—for digitization.

While some libraries are museum-like and vice versa, most librarians will tell you that their job is to make their materials available, not to make interpretations about individual items as museum curators do. Librarians learn what you really want to know through the reference interview and then help you identify and locate appropriate resources. They don't tell you what to read or what to think. Thus, the American Memory project began by limiting interpretative materials about individual items, focusing instead on the provenance of the full digital collection.

IS IT COPYRIGHT FREE?

Because placing the materials themselves on the Web is a form of publishing, one of the first important issues is copyright. The library initially digitized collections that were largely in the public domain, meaning older materials or materials for which the donor had placed no restrictions on use.

Some recently added collections include copyright-protected items for which the library has received permission to include on its American Memory website. For example, while the *Hannah Arendt Papers* are available in their entirety at the Library of Congress and at two other research institutions, only a portion of the full collection is available online. Because a lengthy process would have been necessary to secure permission to release the entire collection, the library concentrated on sections of the papers thought to be most useful for researchers, and those materials are now available in American Memory.

As a publicly supported institution, the library generally does not own rights to material in its collections. Therefore, it does not charge permission fees for use of such material and cannot give or deny permission to publish or otherwise distribute material in its collections. Each American Memory collection has a copyright statement that states what is known about the copyright status of each specific collection. It is the patron's obligation to determine and satisfy copyright or other use restrictions when publishing or otherwise distributing materials found in the library's collections.

IS IT CATALOGED?

A digital item must be cataloged or described in some way if that item is to become truly accessible online. Many of the special collections at the Library of Congress were archival collections that were not cataloged to the item level. For example, manuscripts reside in boxes or containers. The container might be labeled, but the individual items within the container might only be listed by title or number in a "finding aid." Collections selected for digitization early in the project were those for which cataloging information already existed or collections whose finding aids could be adapted for online use.

WILL TECHNOLOGY WORK?

While technology is changing at the speed of light, some archival collections have problems specific to their format. For example, panoramic photographs and some historical maps were too big for the early, first generation scanners. As a result, some selection decisions were postponed, and as the technology evolved, different selection decisions were made. The evolution of technology since 1990, when the Library of Congress first began the American Memory pilot project, also accounts for some technical differences among the collections, which is mentioned in chapter 3.

IS IT UNIQUE OR POPULAR?

Many of the library's special collections contain unique, but infrequently used, materials. These materials of high research value may have limited popular appeal. Other collections contain materials on topics that are less esoteric and, thus, more frequently requested and used. Finding balance on this selection pendulum is a challenge. Arguments can be made for both sides. Because an item is rare or a collection cannot be found elsewhere, digitization will make it more accessible to individual scholars around the world. Conversely, because a collection is requested by so many users, digitization of that collection might be more responsive to user demand.

IS IT SENSITIVE?

When dealing with historical materials, inevitably there will be culturally insensitive materials or materials that may intrude upon an individual's right to privacy. Things *were* different then, and most (but not all) teachers will argue that understanding this difference in cultural customs is part of learning. Most librarians will consider omission of culturally insensitive materials censorship and seek, instead, to present a rich array of materials, representing diverse points of view. Decisions about how to handle materials that fall into these categories must be made before the collection is digitized, and explanation is often provided online. For example, in *Born in Slavery: Narratives from the Federal Writers' Project, 1936–1938,* a note on the language of the narratives discusses problems associated with white stereotypes of "black speech."

IS IT FUNDED?

Because the initial online collections were developed partially with private funding, the donor's wish must be honored. While donors do not create the content, they sometimes specify a collection to be digitized. For example, the AT&T Foundation funded the digitization of the *Alexander Graham Bell Family Papers* (see figure 2-3), a fascinating manuscript collection containing correspondence, notebooks, journals, and photographs documenting Bell's development of the telephone and his interest in deaf education.

AMERICAN MEMORY HISTORICAL COLLECTIONS

With these selection criteria in mind, there are many ways to get familiar with the American Memory collections, but the first caveat to keep in mind is that it takes time—lots of time. In this chapter, you will learn about *kinds* of collections, organized initially by five material formats—*photographs, written materials, recorded sound, maps,* and *motion pictures.* Examples are provided for each category, but keep in mind that there are numerous collections in each category and some collections provide multiple formats of materials.

Not only does it take time to get familiar with the content of the American Memory collections, it is an iterative process. You have to come at it from various directions. Knowing the content intellectually is not like knowing how the content relates to your instructional needs. Thus, along with collection descriptions, in this chapter you will learn about instructional techniques and workshops that transport these materials into a K–12 setting.

When you see these materials, you may be filled with all kinds of ideas of how to use them. Or, if you have never used primary sources, you may want some ideas to jumpstart your thinking process. While some examples of lesson plans and activities are given in this chapter, in subsequent chapters you will learn more about how elementary, middle school, and high school teachers are using the American Memory collections in their classrooms. Understanding the impact of these materials on creative instruction is what is so compelling. Once you do, you will be hooked!

The collections that are highlighted in this section are representative of the more than 100 now available on the Library of Congress American Memory website. To view a list of all available collections, go to the American Memory home page and select Collection Finder, which is discussed more fully in chapter 3 (see figure 3-1 on page 41). There you will find a list of all collections, collections listed by topics, and collections listed by formats. The descriptions that follow are taken directly from the website and they are included to whet your appetite. There is no substitute for going online and exploring independently!

Photographs and Prints

Particularly for this generation, pictures communicate in a way text does not; today's students are highly visual. Teachers who have used historical photographs suggest that photographs are often the easiest way to draw students into historical inquiry activities. Prints and photographs can be used effectively by even the youngest students.

Figures 2-7 and 2-8 show a typical photo for use with children and a photo analysis worksheet. With photographs, as with other formats of materials, students must be taught analytical skills. They must be taught how "to read" an image—how to determine the difference between what they know, what they think they know, and what more they need to know to understand the photograph or print. The photo analysis worksheet that is reproduced here is from the

What Do You See:
Photo Analysis Guide

What Do You See?	Photo Analysis Guide	Activities
Observation	**Knowledge**	**Interpretation**
Describe exactly what you see in the photo. What people and objects are shown? How are they arranged? What is the physical setting? What other details can you see?	Summarize what you already know about the situation and time period shown, and the people and objects that appear.	Say what you conclude from what you see. What's going on in the picture? Who are the people and what are they doing? What might be the function of the objects? What can we conclude about the time period?
Further Research: What questions has the photo raised? What are some sources you can use to find answers?		

Figure 2-7
Children must be taught visual literacy skills to understand historical photographs.
This photo-analysis guide is one of many teaching tools available on the Learning Page
to help teachers structure this process.

"Discovering American Memory Workshop" on the Learning Page.[3] This and other worksheets will be helpful to your students who are working with visual materials, and all can be found on the Learning Page. Refer to the sidebar for examples of American Memory photographic and print collections of particular interest to K–12 educators.

You will find dozens of lesson plans on the Learning Page that focus on images from a variety of American Memory collections. Many teachers find that historical images provide wonderful cues for creative writing assignments. For example, a lesson designed for middle school students requires students to find a photograph of a Civil War battle, do some research, and then write a short eye-witness newspaper account.[4]

Figure 2-8
Chilkat children on river bank, Klukwan, Alaska, 1894. Photograph by John Francis Pratt. From *American Indians of the Pacific Northwest*, American Memory collection, contributed by University of Washington Libraries.

Examples of American Memory Print & Photograph Collections

Excerpted from http://memory.loc.gov

Title: *Baseball Cards, 1887–1914*

Description: This collection presents 2,100 early baseball cards dating from 1887 to 1914. The cards show such legendary figures as Ty Cobb stealing third base for Detroit, Tris Speaker batting for Boston, and pitcher Cy Young posing formally in his Cleveland uniform. Other notable players include Connie Mack, Walter Johnson, King Kelly, and Christy Mathewson.

Title: *By Popular Demand: Votes for Women Suffrage*

Description: A selection of 38 pictures including portraits of many individuals, photographs of suffrage parades, picketing suffragists, and an anti-suffrage display, as well as cartoons commenting on the movement.

Title: *Civil War Treasures from the New-York Historical Society*

Description: The images in this collection are drawn from the New-York Historical Society's rich archival collections documenting the Civil War. They include recruiting posters for New York City regiments of volunteers, stereographic views demonstrating the mustering of soldiers and of popular support for the Union in New York City, photography showing the war's impact, both in the North and South, and drawings and writings by ordinary soldiers on both sides.

Title: *History of the American West, 1860–1920: Photographs from the Collection of the Denver Public Library*

Description: Over 30,000 photographs illuminate many aspects of the history of the American West. They illustrate Colorado towns and landscape, document the place of mining in the history of Colorado and the West, and show the lives of Native Americans from more than forty tribes living west of the Mississippi River. Also included are World War II photographs of the 10th Mountain Division, ski troops based in Colorado who saw action in Italy.

Written Materials

Materials in this category include books, manuscripts, pamphlets, interviews, printed ephemera, and even song sheets and sheet music—a wide range of materials, many of which are not commonly found in school libraries. See figure 2-9, for example, for a delightful poem written by Helen Keller, who with the help of Alexander Graham Bell came to "see" the natural world in a remarkable way. Look as well at the letter (figure 2-10) from Mary Todd Lincoln to her husband, who at the time was on the Antietam battlefield. In this four-page letter, she gently chides President Lincoln for not being more decisive in regard to General

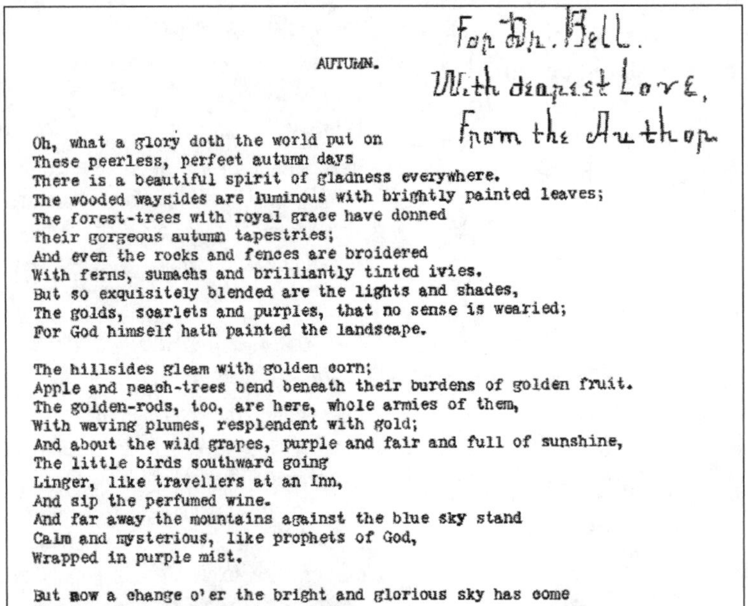

For Dr. Bell.
With deepest Love,
From the Author

AUTUMN.

Oh, what a glory doth the world put on
These peerless, perfect autumn days
There is a beautiful spirit of gladness everywhere.
The wooded waysides are luminous with brightly painted leaves;
The forest-trees with royal grace have donned
Their gorgeous autumn tapestries;
And even the rocks and fences are broidered
With ferns, sumachs and brilliantly tinted ivies.
But so exquisitely blended are the lights and shades,
The golds, scarlets and purples, that no sense is wearied;
For God himself hath painted the landscape.

The hillsides gleam with golden corn;
Apple and peach-trees bend beneath their burdens of golden fruit.
The golden-rods, too, are here, whole armies of them,
With waving plumes, resplendent with gold;
And about the wild grapes, purple and fair and full of sunshine,
The little birds southward going
Linger, like travellers at an Inn,
And sip the perfumed wine.
And far away the mountains against the blue sky stand
Calm and mysterious, like prophets of God,
Wrapped in purple mist.

But now a change o'er the bright and glorious sky has come
The threatening clouds stand still,
The silent skies are dark and solemn;
The mists of morning hide the golden face of day.
And a mysterious hand has stripped the trees;
And with rustle and whir the leaves descend,
And like little frightened birds
Lie trembling on the ground.
Bare and sad the forest-monarchs stand
Like kings of eld, all their splendor swept away.

And down from his ice-bound realm in the North
Comes Winter, with snowy locks, and tear-drops frozen on his cheeks;
For he is the brother of Death, and acquainted with Sorrow.
Autumn sees him from afar,
And, as a child to her father runneth,
She to the protecting arms of kindly Winter fleeth;
And in his mantle of snow
Tenderly he folds her lovely form,
And on his breast she falls asleep
Ere yet the storm-winds have loosed their fury
Upon a white and silent world.

She sleeps unconscious of the sorrow that must be,
And dreams perchance of sylvan music,
And the splendor that was, and will again be hers;
For Autumn dies not 'Tis as the Poet says:
"There is no Death. What seems so is transition."
All that is divine lives
In some nobler sphere, some fairer form.

Helen Keller

Hulton, Penn., Oct 27th, 1893.

Figure 2-9
This typewritten poem by Helen Keller, deaf and blind since she was nineteen months old, paints an amazingly vivid picture of nature's abundance. Helen wrote this poem for Alexander Graham Bell when she was thirteen; the poem is found in the American Memory collection *Words and Deeds*.

McClellan. First-person accounts—written or spoken—are of particular interest to students. You will learn more about this in chapter 6.

Examples of American Memory collections containing written materials of interest to K–12 educators are shown on page 28. Note that although many of these collections also contain visual materials, they are still considered "text." Students may need help with vocabulary words and with establishing the historical context to understand the text. Consult the section titled "How Does It Read?" in the Discovering American Memory workshop for tips on getting started.[5]

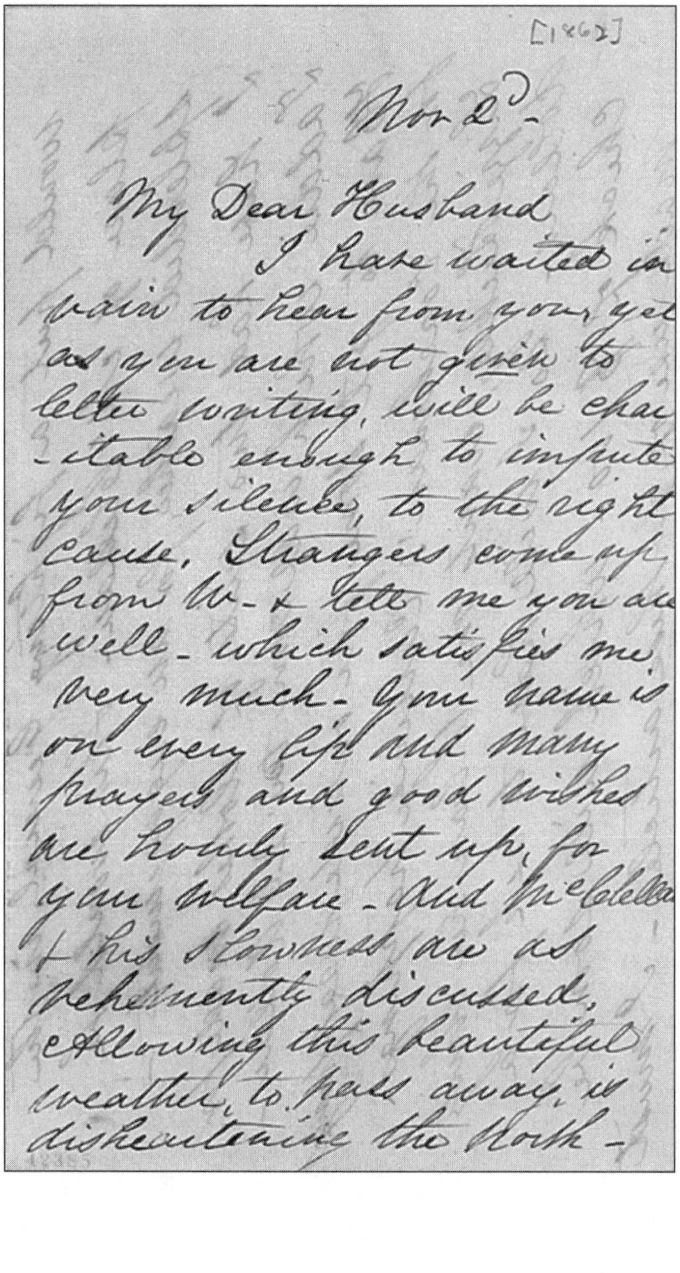

[1862]
Nov 2d -
My Dear Husband
I have waited in
vain to hear from you, yet
as you are not given to
letter writing, will be char
-itable enough to impute
your silence, to the right
cause, Strangers come up
from W- & tell me you are
well - which satisfies me
very much - Your name is
on every lip and many
prayers and good wishes
are hourly sent up, for
your welfare - And McClellan
& his slowness are as
vehemently discussed,
Allowing this beautiful
weather, to pass away, is
disheartening the North -

Figure 2-10
This handwritten letter by Mary Todd Lincoln to her husband advises him to remove the hesitant General McClellan from command. From *Words and Deeds*, American Memory collection.

For an innovative use of digital text materials, go to the Learning Page and find the lesson plan section. Look at "Marco Polo's Travels on the Erie Canal." This lesson designed for grades 4–6 uses a book found online as the kernel of many activities associated with learning about the economic and social impact of the Erie Canal. American Memory ephemera materials, song sheets, and sheet music complement this lesson.[6]

Examples of American Memory Text Collections

Excerpted from http://memory.loc.gov

Title: *An American Time Capsule: Three Centuries of Broadsides and Other Printed Ephemera*

Description: The Printed Ephemera collection at the Library of Congress is a rich repository of Americana. In total, the collection comprises 28,000 primary-source items dating from the seventeenth century to the present and encompassing key events and eras in American history. Among them are a variety of posters, notices, invitations, proclamations, leaflets, propaganda, manifestos, menus, and business cards. They capture the experience of the Revolutionary War, slavery, the western land rush, the Civil War, Women's Suffrage, and the Industrial Revolution from the viewpoint of those who lived through them.

Title: *Born in Slavery: Slave Narratives from the Federal Writers' Project, 1936–1938*

Description: The collection contains more than 2,300 first-person accounts of slavery and 500 black-and-white photographs of former slaves. These narratives were collected in the 1930s as part of the Federal Writers' Project of the Works Progress Administration (WPA) and assembled and microfilmed in 1941 as the seventeen-volume *Slave Narratives: A Folk History of Slavery in the United States from Interviews with Former Slaves.*

Title: *George Washington Papers at the Library of Congress, 1741–1799*

Description: The online version of the George Washington Papers at the Library of Congress offers access to the complete collection from the Library's Manuscript Division. This consists of approximately 65,000 items (176,000 pages). Correspondence, letterbooks, commonplace books, diaries and journals, reports, notes, financial account books, and military papers accumulated by George Washington from 1741 through 1799 are organized into eight series, which will be published successively.

Title: *"I Do Solemnly Swear . . .": Presidential Inaugurations*

Description: The collection brings together approximately 400 items or 2,000 digital files from each of the 63 inaugurations from George Washington's in 1789 to George W. Bush's in 2001. This presentation includes diaries and letters of presidents and of those who witnessed inaugurations, handwritten drafts of inaugural addresses, broadsides, inaugural tickets and programs, prints, photographs, and sheet music. The collection has been organized chronologically by presidential inauguration and an effort has been made to offer a balanced number of items for each inaugural event.

Title: *We'll Sing to Abe Our Song! Sheet Music about Lincoln, Emancipation, and the Civil War*

Description: The collection includes more than 200 sheet-music compositions that represent Lincoln and the Civil War as reflected in popular music. It spans the years from Lincoln's presidential campaign in 1859 through the centenary of Lincoln's birth in 1909.

Title: *Words and Deeds in American History: Selected Documents Celebrating the Manuscript Division's First 100 Years*

Description: In honor of the Manuscript Division's centennial, the staff has selected for online display approximately ninety representative documents spanning from the fifteenth century to the mid-twentieth century. Included are the papers of presidents, cabinet ministers, members of Congress, Supreme Court justices, military officers and diplomats, reformers and political activists, artists and writers, scientists and inventors, and other prominent Americans whose lives reflect our country's evolution.

Recorded Sound

What teenager will not relate to sound? Materials in this category include ethnographic recordings, interviews, speeches, musical presentations, and the like. To get students to listen critically, begin with the "What Do You Hear" exercise in the "Discovering American Memory" self-serve workshop on the Learning Page.[7] The examples of American Memory sound recordings given below are of particular interest to K–12 educators.

Maps

Most of us think of maps as geographical locators, but maps are also historical documents that personalize history, illustrate change over time, and document contemporary culture. They can be very useful with other forms of primary sources to set the context and the physical environment as it was known at the time. There are maps that depict cities and towns, wilderness areas, military battles, transportation routes, Native American settlements, population migration, and much, much more. For example, figure 2-11 shows the city of Boston as depicted by Currier and Ives in 1873.

Examples of American Memory Recorded Sound Collections

Excerpted from http://memory.loc.gov

Title: *After the Day of Infamy: "Man-on-the-Street" Interviews Following the Attack on Pearl Harbor*

Description: This collection contains twelve hours of opinions recorded following the bombing of Pearl Harbor from over two hundred individuals across the United States.

Title: *American Leaders Speak: Recordings from World War II and the 1920 Election*

Description: The Nation's Forum Collection from the Motion Picture, Broadcasting, and Recorded Sound Division consists of fifty-nine sound recordings of speeches by American leaders at the turn of the century. The speeches focus on issues and events surrounding the First World War and the subsequent presidential election of 1920.

Title: *Emile Berliner and the Birth of the Recording Industry*

Description: Emile Berliner and the Birth of the Recording Industry is a selection of more than 400 items from the Emile Berliner Papers and 108 Berliner sound recordings from the Library of Congress's Motion Picture, Broadcasting and Recorded Sound Division. Berliner (1851–1929) was responsible for the development of the microphone and the flat recording disc and gramophone player. Spanning the years 1870 to 1956, the collection comprises correspondence, articles, lectures, speeches, scrapbooks, photographs, catalogs, clippings, experiment notes, and rare sound recordings.

Title: *Tending the Commons: Folklife and Landscape in Southern West Virginia*

Description: The collection incorporates 958 excerpts from original sound recordings and 1,270 photographs documenting traditional uses of the mountains in Southern West Virginia's Big Coal River Valley. Functioning as a de facto commons, the mountains have supported a way of life that for many generations has entailed hunting, gathering, and subsistence gardening, as well as coal mining and timbering. The collection includes extensive interviews on native forest species and the seasonal round of traditional harvesting (including spring greens; summer berries and fish; and fall nuts, roots such as ginseng, fruits, and game) and documents community cultural events such as storytelling, baptisms in the river, cemetery customs, and the spring "ramp" feasts.

Figure 2-11
This pictorial view of the city of Boston was done by Currier & Ives in 1873. Panoramic maps such as this one were drawn from an oblique angle, often for promotional purposes. This map is found in *Panoramic Maps, 1847–1929*, American Memory collection.

For an excellent introduction to maps, consult the Learning Page activity "Zoom into Maps."[8] It is especially important to explore the map collections online because you can "zoom" in and out to get a more detailed view. In fact, this is one example in which digital technology *enhances* the materials by enabling the user to get a closer look than is possible with the naked eye. The chart below lists examples of American Memory map collections of particular interest to K–12 educators.

Examples of American Memory Map Collections

Excerpted from http://memory.loc.gov

Title: *The American Revolution and Its Era: Maps and Charts of North America and the West Indies, 1750–1789*

Description: The maps and charts in this collection number well over two 2,000 different items, with easily as many or more unnumbered duplicates, many with distinct colorations and annotations. Almost 600 maps are original manuscript drawings.

Title: *Civil War Maps*

Description: The Civil War Map collection of the Geography and Map Division consists of reconnaissance, sketch, coastal, and theater-of-war maps that depict troop activities and fortifications during the Civil War. Part of this selection contains maps by Major Jedediah Hotchkiss, a topographical engineer in the Confederate Army. Hotchkiss made detailed battle maps that were used by Generals Lee and Jackson. This selection also includes maps that depict General Sherman's military campaigns in Tennessee, Mississippi, Georgia, and the Carolinas.

Title: *Panoramic Maps*

Description: Panoramic maps are idealized schematic views of American towns and cities produced during the nineteenth and early twentieth centuries. Although not generally drawn to scale, they show street patterns, individual buildings, and major landscape features in perspective.

Title: *Railroad Maps, 1828–1900*

Description: Railroad maps represent an important historical record, illustrating the growth of travel and settlement as well as the development of industry and agriculture in the United States. They depict the development of cartographic style and technique as well as highlighting the achievement of early railroaders. Included in the collection are progress report surveys for individual lines, official government surveys, promotional maps, maps showing land grants and rights-of-way, and route guides published by commercial firms. All of the items presented here are documented in *Railroad Maps of the United States*, compiled by Andrew M. Modelski in 1975, an annotated bibliography of 623 maps held by the Geography and Map Division.

Some teachers like to use maps as a jumping-off point or as a visual organizer for a larger investigation. Look, for example, at a lesson plan using maps that appears on the Learning Page. "Mapping My Spot in History" uses a 1903 map of Dover, New Jersey, and asks students to create a contemporary map of their own town and their blocks in a style reminiscent of turn-of-the-century panoramic maps.[9]

To supplement current events activities, consult "Places in the News." This special online presentation by the Library of Congress Map Division highlights current hot spots in the world.

Motion Pictures

Motion pictures are, perhaps, the ultimate form of multimedia content relevant to today's students. But, this is "film" in the way they least expect. Most of the motion picture films are black-and-white, silent, and record everyday life, as in figure 2-12, which shows immigrants arriving at Ellis Island.

Many films are a part of the Paper Print Collection at the Library of Congress. Prior to 1912, there was no copyright protection for film, so producers sent their film as paper contact prints to the Copyright Office at the Library of Congress. Some of the online films have been reassembled from the paper prints. The digital files are very large and thus take more time to download than many other resources. They can, however, be downloaded and saved to the hard drive for more convenient offline classroom use. Refer to page 32 for examples of American Memory motion picture collections of particular interest to K–12 educators.

RELATED PRIMARY SOURCE MATERIALS

While the focus of this book is on the American Memory Historical Collections, there are a number of other digital initiatives at the Library of Congress that are related and may be of considerable interest to K–12 educators.

Figure 2-12
These images are taken from the paper print collection and show immigrants arriving at Ellis Island. See these and other films in *Life of a City: Early Films of New York, 1898–1906*, American Memory collection.

Examples of American Memory Motion Picture Collections

Excerpted from http://memory.loc.gov

Title: *America at Work, America at Leisure, Motion Pictures from 1849 to 1915*

Description: This collection of motion pictures features work, school, and leisure activities in the United States from 1894 to 1915. Highlights include films of the United States Postal Service from 1903, cattle breeding, firefighters, ice manufacturing, logging, calisthenic and gymnastic exercises in schools, amusement parks, boxing, expositions, football, parades, swimming, and other sporting events.

Title: *The Life of a City: Early Films of New York, 1898–1906*

Description: This collection contains forty-five films of New York City dating from 1898 to 1906 from the Paper Print Collection of the Library of Congress. Of these, twenty-five were made by the American Mutoscope and Biograph Company, while the remaining twenty are Edison Company productions.

Title: *Inside an American Factory: Films of the Westinghouse Works, 1904*

Description: The collection contains twenty-one actuality films showing various views of Westinghouse factories in 1904. Most prominently featured are the Westinghouse Air Brake Company, the Westinghouse Electric and Manufacturing Company, and the Westinghouse Machine Company. The films were intended to showcase the company's operations. Exterior and interior shots of the factories are shown along with scenes of male and female workers performing their duties at the plants.

Title: *Theodore Roosevelt: His Life and Times on Film*

Description: Theodore Roosevelt was the first U.S. president to have his career and life chronicled on a large scale by motion picture companies. This presentation features 104 films that record events in Roosevelt's life, from the Spanish-American War in 1898 to his death in 1919. Besides containing scenes of Roosevelt, these films include views of world figures, politicians, monarchs, and friends and family members of Roosevelt who influenced his life and the era in which he lived. There are also four sound recordings made by Roosevelt for the Edison Company in 1912 in which he states his progressive political views.

Prints and Photographs Online Catalog

The Prints and Photographs Division of the Library of Congress has been involved with automation and digitization projects from the very beginning. Its catalog was designed for in-house researchers, but it is now available on the Web (http://lcweb2.loc.gov/pp/pphome.html). Cataloging records describe collections, groups of images, and individual items. Some of the records have associated digital images. Because of possible copyright concerns, many of these digital images are only available as "thumbnails" when accessed outside the library, but even these images can be useful to educators. If you visit this electronic catalog, you will see that some collections are also included in the American Memory Historical Collections.

Global Gateway

As the world gets both bigger and smaller, access to international materials is becoming increasingly important for historical and cultural understanding. Because the Library of Congress collects materials in 460 languages, the Global Gateway can be viewed as an extension of the American Memory project. It currently provides primary sources in two collections: *Meeting of the Frontiers*, available in English and Russian, and *Historias Paralelas*, available in English and

Spanish. Each digital collection is a collaborative project, the first a collaboration of the Library of Congress and the National Library of Russia, the Russian State Library, and the Rasmuson Library at the University of Alaska, Fairbanks; the second is a collaboration between the Library of Congress and the National Library of Spain. Each collection is built around the concept of America's frontiers and the blending of cultures.

This area is expected to grow. More projects are in the pipeline, notably one with Brazil and another with the Netherlands.

Exhibitions

The online exhibits from the Library of Congress provide great primary source materials for the busy teacher (see figure 2-13). Available from the Library of Congress home page, these exhibitions were once part of larger displays shown at the Library of Congress in Washington, D.C. Beginning in 1994, portions of the exhibits were digitized for online presentation. Not all items in the exhibitions were, or are, held at the Library of Congress. Some items were on loan from other institutions for the purpose of the physical exhibitions and later digitized for the online galleries.

While these interpretive exhibits showcasing primary sources were planned for adult visitors to the library, many of the exhibits, including those listed on page 34, are useful to K–12 educators. The descriptions of the exhibits have been excerpted from the Library of Congress Exhibitions website. These online galleries can bring the resources and the services of the Library of Congress to interested

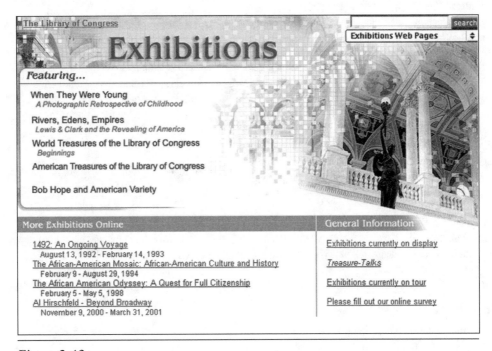

Figure 2-13
The online exhibitions provide interpretative background about selected Library of Congress primary-source materials.

Examples of Library of Congress Online Exhibitions

Excerpted from http://www.loc.gov/exhibits/

Title: *1492: An Ongoing Voyage*

Description: This exhibition examines contact between American people and European explorers, conquerors, and settlers from 1492 to 1600. The dramatic events following 1492 set the stage for numerous cultural interactions in the Americas, which are still in progress—a complex and ongoing voyage.

Title: *The African-American Mosaic: African-American Culture and History*

Description: This exhibition extracts materials published by the Library of Congress in a book of the same name highlighting African-American materials in the library's collection. Other exhibit materials, not specifically described in the publication, are also included to illustrate that the Mosaic is an effective guide to the library's rich collections, not an exhaustive inventory.

Title: *The African American Odyssey: A Quest for Full Citizenship*

Description: This exhibition showcases the library's African-American collections, including a wide array of important and rare books, government documents, manuscripts, maps, musical scores, plays, films, and recordings.

Title: *American Treasures of the Library of Congress*

Description: This exhibit features unique items from the Library of Congress that curators have chosen as the library's top "treasures." The exhibit is organized into three sections—memory, reason, and imagination—just as Thomas Jefferson arranged his personal library.

Title: *Declaring Independence: Drafting the Documents*

Description: This exhibit highlights documents and prints held by the Library of Congress that tell the story of the founding of our nation.

Title: *The Gettysburg Address*

Description: This exhibit highlights the various drafts of Lincoln's Gettysburg Address and includes the only known photograph of President Lincoln at Gettysburg.

Title: *Language of the Land: Journeys into Literary America*

Description: Using the metaphor of a journey, *Language of the Land: Journeys into Literary America* examines the nation's literary heritage through maps, photographs, and the works of American authors from a variety of periods.

Title: *Madison's Treasures*

Description: This exhibition presents significant documents from the Library of Congress's James Madison collection, most of which relate to the drafting of the Constitution and the introduction of the Bill of Rights. Other documents relate to the freedom of religion and to the burning of Washington, D.C., by the British in 1814—perhaps the major embarrassment of Madison's political career.

Title: *Temple of Liberty: Building the Capitol for a New Nation*

Description: This exhibition documents the design, architecture, and symbols used to build a capitol for the new nation.

Title: *Thomas Jefferson*

Description: This exhibition traces Jefferson's intellectual development from his earliest days in the Piedmont to an ever-expanding realm of influence in republican Virginia, the American Revolutionary government, the creation of the American nation, and the revolution in individual rights in America and the world. It provides a Jefferson timeline and information about his library.

Title: *Women Come to the Front: Journalists, Photographers and Broadcasters from WWII*

Description: This exhibition tells the story of eight American women whose work documented the war. Their stories—drawn from private papers and photographs primarily in Library of Congress collections—open a window on a generation of women who changed American society forever by securing a place for themselves in the workplace, in the newsroom, and on the battlefield.

students. The Madison exhibit, for example, was based on a one-day symposium for scholars held at the Library of Congress. An online link to a cybercast of that symposium allows K–12 students to see and hear scholars discuss important issues.

Fun Stuff for Kids and Families

TODAY IN HISTORY

Available from the American Memory home page, Today in History highlights selected content from the American Memory collections that occurred or relate to the current date (see figure 2-14). You can search the archive by keyword, date, or month. Asking children to research their birthday is an easy way to get them involved.

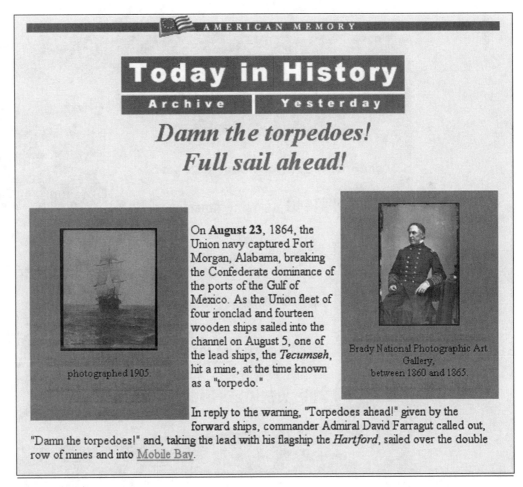

Figure 2-14
Today in History is a daily feature that uses primary sources to highlight events that occurred on that particular day in history.

AMERICA'S LIBRARY

America's Library was designed with children and parents in mind. It tells history through stories—stories of amazing Americans; of places and events; of disasters, devastation, and destruction; of leisure-time activities, like games, dance, music, and song. The stories chosen are illustrated with primary sources, and if more information is desired, online links direct you to more stories and primary-source materials (see figure 2-15).

Stories are also enhanced through interactive activities. Children can send a "postcard" linking an item from the Library of Congress collections with a personal e-mail message. Children can find stories that "happened" on their birthday. Stories about the fifty states are easily accessible and fun for young children to explore through the interactive Treasure Hunt activity. America's Library is meant to be interactively explored, and some elementary teachers may find activities of interest to their students although they are not necessarily curriculum related. The Learning Page "links" to America's Library.

Figure 2-15
America's Library is designed to help children and families to learn more about history through primary sources and the stories they evoke.

Because it was designed for home use, the site designers created it so that children and parents would not get lost in the larger Library of Congress site. Thus, there is no return loop to American Memory or the Learning Page, which is a limitation for school use.

WISE GUIDE

The Wise Guide, begun in October 2002, is an interactive online magazine highlighting digital items from the Library of Congress's many online collections, presentations, and exhibitions. Each month a new issue is published; old issues are archived and available for use.

LIBRARIAN-TEACHER PARTNERSHIPS

Becoming familiar with the American Memory collections, online exhibits, and the other digital presentations from the Library of Congress is a daunting task. Locating them is not always as easy as it would first seem because different divisions of the library produce various sections, and, thus, they appear in different parts of the Library of Congress website.

Understanding the American Memory collections alone is intimidating to some educators—if only because of the sheer numbers. The material is sophisticated, and understanding it requires considerable background knowledge. Knowing what to do with the materials requires creativity—and time.

And, then, there's the technical side. Using the collections requires computer expertise: navigating the Web and manipulating computer files. It definitely involves understanding how to search online. While the American Memory collections are organized in a similar fashion, once you get involved you will discover that some collections may be arranged a little differently and have slightly different search capabilities. This is discussed in some detail in chapter 3.

If ever there were a resource that *demands* that teachers and librarians work together, this is it. Librarians, take it upon yourselves to get familiar with this website and encourage your teachers to come into the library to plan. Teachers, if you need help searching the collections, see your school library media specialist. Even if he or she is not familiar with this website, school librarians and media specialists understand the concepts of online searching and soon will be up to speed. Here is a wonderful opportunity begging for collaborative teaching and creative learning.

NOTES

1. James H. Billington, "Culture, Computers, and Content," September 9, 1999.
2. From letter to Samuel H. Smith, September 21, 1814 [online], available from http://www.loc.gov/exhibits/jefferson/images/vc219p1.jpg.
3. "What Do You See?" This photo-analysis guide is a part of "Discovering American Memory," an online self-serve workshop on the Learning Page, available from http://memory.loc.gov/ammem/ndlpedu/educators/workshop/discover/yousee.html.

4. Amy Donnelly and Elizabeth Ridgway, "Matthew Brady Bunch: Civil War Newspapers" [online], 1997, available from http://memory.loc.gov/ammem/ndlpedu/lessons/98/brady/home.html.

5. "How Does It Read?" This journalistic guide is part of "Discovering American Memory," an online self-serve workshop on the Learning Page, available from http://memory.loc.gov/ammem/ndlpedu/educators/workshop/discover/read.html.

6. Janet Williammee and Rhonda King, "Marco Polo's Travels on the Erie Canal: An Educational Journey" [online], 2000, available from: http://memory.loc.gov/ammen/ndlpedu/lessons/00/canal.

7. "What Do You Hear?" This listening guide is a part of "Discovering American Memory," an online self-serve workshop on the Learning Page, available from http://memory.loc.gov/ammem/ndlpedu/educators/workshop/discover/hear.html.

8. "Zoom into Maps" is a Learning Page activity that provides a comprehensive introduction to using maps with students, available from http://memory.loc.gov/ammem/ndlpedu/features/maps/index.html.

9. Judy Klement and Elizabeth Clark, "Mapping My Spot in History" [online], 2001, available from http://memory.loc.gov/ammem/ndlpedu/lessons/01/map/overview.html.

CHAPTER THREE

Finding Materials Online

How do you get started exploring this vast archive of primary-source materials from the Library of Congress? I'm reminded of the feeling I often have when I get on an elevator in the Library of Congress and push the button for the sixth floor. I go back to my own thoughts and the elevator stops. I step out, thinking, of course, that it is the sixth floor because that is the button I pushed. But, things look a little unfamiliar. It's almost the same, but not exactly. Whoops! It's the third floor and someone else is getting *on* the elevator also wanting to go to the sixth floor. My orientation is off for just a few seconds until I realize what has happened. Not everyone wants to go directly to the sixth floor!

Finding your way around a large library is similar to searching a massive website. There are many ways to get to where you want to go. Some are more direct than others. It depends upon how much time you have, what you need to do, and how you best learn. There are also many places you *should* go, but may not know about. How do you learn about specialized places of interest? There is no "one size fits all" in terms of getting acquainted with this website. The Library of Congress website is designed so that many people can hop on and off the elevator at different times and find items of interest.

This chapter describes how you can explore the vastness of American Memory Historical Collections and then describes the Learning Page—the elevator stop especially designed for teachers. The chapter concludes with a discussion of the nuances of searching American Memory.

As educators, the first thing you need to keep in mind is that the Library of Congress is a national research library and its collections reflect this broad constituency. Its vast collections were not acquired with the specific needs of the K–12 educational community in mind. Some of the online collections, however, were selected for digitization (particularly through the LC/Ameritech competition) because of their potential interest to K–12 educators.

Note that the Library of Congress home page (see figure 2-1) has a section that directs online users to different parts of the website depending upon who they are. "Especially for Teachers" will take you to the Learning Page. The Learning Page is a companion website to the Library's digital offerings most of which—but not all—reside in the American Memory Historical Collections. Let's come back here after first looking at other pathways that may be of special interest to *all* librarians—including school library media specialists.

For school library media specialists, the first step in getting acquainted with an online website is to know the scope and depth of the content. While there are a myriad of pathways to exploration, keep in mind that understanding this website is all about the collections. Whatever elevator button you push will ultimately lead you to one of the digitized collections or to individual items from the collections that reside, with few exceptions, at the Library of Congress.

ESPECIALLY FOR LIBRARIANS

Collection Finder—First Stop

As discussed in the previous chapter, using the Collection Finder (figure 3-1) is a good way for some people—especially librarians—to start learning about the scope of the American Memory Historical Collections. As noted earlier, the Collection Finder is currently accessible from the American Memory home page. (See figure 2-2.) Keep in mind that web design is constantly evolving, so this navigational feature may change in the future.

You can browse all collections or choose collections by format (as well as broad topic, time, place, or *digital* format). The default arrangement of these lists is by keyword; thus related collections are clustered together. Included is a shortened title. To get a better sense of the content of the collections, click on the "Show descriptions" link on the right side of the screen. This will provide fuller descriptions, similar to those reproduced in chapter 2. Warning: With more than 100 collections online, this will take considerable time, even if you just review the online descriptions. It is, however, the rare librarian who can resist following the links that go directly into the full collection. If you do this, order out for pizza. You'll be busy for hours! But, if you are a detailed, linear thinker, this may be just the right approach. Most of the American Memory collections are fully searchable in at least two ways: a system-level search across all American Memory collections and a collection-level search. These two approaches to searching are discussed in more detail later in this chapter.

Exhibitions—Second Stop

Unfortunately, the Collection Finder does not find the exhibitions, that is, the online galleries that include examples of primary sources set in context. Exhibitions are accessible from the Library of Congress home page, but they are not currently searchable in the same way as American Memory collections. (See figure 2-13.) Exhibits are designed like coffee-table books—glossy publications to be savored

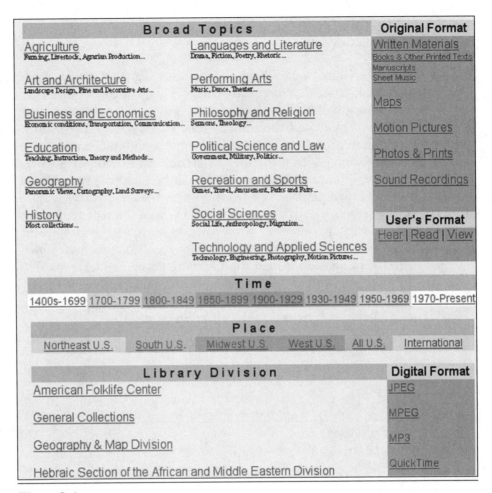

Figure 3-1
Use the Collection Finder to explore American Memory collections
by format, broad subject area, or time period.

leisurely, page by page. Online exhibitions are listed alphabetically by title, and because there are fewer exhibitions than American Memory collections, you can browse the list quickly. While there is no expandable list with short descriptions like there is with American Memory's Collection Finder, there is a simple cross-exhibit search feature. You will find this in the upper right-hand corner of your computer screen.

The discerning librarian will note that some online exhibitions are also included in the American Memory collections. "Hmm . . . ," I hear you thinking. "I thought the American Memory collections did not include interpretative materials." In the course of time, American Memory selection criteria were amended to include some interpretive materials and materials selected from archival collections. To make these museum-like presentations more accessible to the general public, they were wrapped into the American Memory collections where they have enhanced search features.

ESPECIALLY FOR TEACHERS: THE LEARNING PAGE

While the Global Gateway and many other digital resources described in chapter 2 are fascinating, the American Memory Historical Collections and the Online Exhibitions will be the primary focus for K–12 educators. American Memory is where you will find the mother lode of digital primary-source materials. The Exhibitions are where you will find some useful interpretive material and selected primary sources. To make these materials more accessible to K–12 educators, in 1996 the Library of Congress designed the Learning Page (figure 3-2).

The Learning Page is a front door to the American Memory collections that is designed especially for teachers and school library media specialists who want to use primary sources or want to learn more about using primary sources with their students. All American Memory collections and some exhibitions are directly accessible through the Learning Page. The Learning Page has seven sections: getting started, lesson plans, features and activities, collection connections, community center, professional development, and news. A brief description of each section is provided in the chart on page 43.

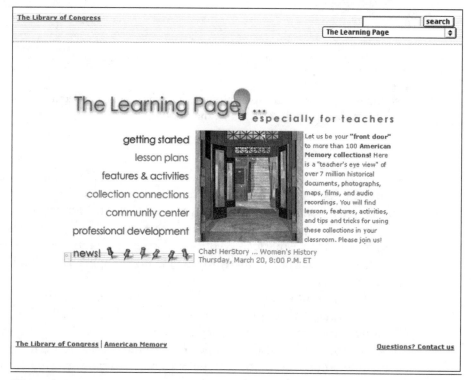

Figure 3-2
The Learning Page, designed for K–12 teachers and media specialists, is the "front door" to the American Memory collections.

How to Get Started

How best to proceed depends upon how much time you have and what you need to do. If you are a busy teacher looking for material on a specific topic to use *now,* the features and activities are a good place to start. What teacher would not like to find ready-made materials on immigration, elections, inaugurations, first ladies, holidays, women pioneers—and lots of interactive activities that draw upon primary source materials? But, keep in mind you will only find a dozen or so specific topics developed. Just because you do not find a feature or activity on a specific topic, it does not mean that appropriate primary-source materials on that topic do not exist in American Memory. It just means you need to work a little harder to locate them.

Using the Library of Congress Learning Page

http://www.loc.gov/learn

Getting Started: If you are a new user, start here. In this section, you will find simple contextual information about the function of the Learning Page and how it relates to the American Memory collections. You will find basic information about primary sources and links to search strategies and tools, including the pathfinder indices mentioned earlier.

Lesson Plans: Here you will find dozens of teacher-created lesson plans, most of which are products of the American Memory Fellows Program, which was discussed briefly in chapter 2. These lessons can be used "as is" or adapted for your own classroom requirements. You will also find more in-depth information about primary sources and how to design a lesson using primary sources.

Features and Activities: Here you will find exhibition-like online galleries designed especially for K–12 use. They bring together items from across the many American Memory collections on curricular themes that are commonly taught in K–12 schools—elections, inaugurations, national holidays, immigration, and others. Many are interactive and require computers with multimedia capability.

Collection Connections: While the Features and Activities provide context on topics for the busy teacher, the Collection Connections provide curricular context for individual collections. These materials highlight themes that are represented in the collection with links to individual items. Guiding

questions are posed for historical inquiry, critical thinking, and language arts activities. A summary-of-resources page guides you to special presentations and indices within the collection, to other collections, and to exhibitions of interest and also provides references to other resources—bibliographies, collections, and exhibits at the Library of Congress.

Community Center: Here is an electronic meeting place for educators to discuss the use of primary sources in the curriculum. You can read and contribute to an online newsletter, The Source. You can participate in regularly scheduled online chats with library staff on monthly themes, and join an online notification list of new collections and Learning Page content.

Professional Development: Here you will find workshops you can attend at the Library of Congress: self-paced, self-serve workshops for independent use and videoconference workshops available for scheduling in your district. You will also find handouts prepared by Library of Congress staff that you can use if you are designing your own workshop for colleagues. These opportunities are discussed more fully in chapter 8.

News! This is a bulletin board announcing upcoming conference presentations and Learning Page activities and events.

THE AMERICAN MEMORY TIMELINE

If you are a history teacher or want to develop an assignment that requires historical context, you may want to begin by looking at the first feature on the Learning Page, the American Memory Timeline (figure 3-3). This is most useful for middle school and high school teachers. Here you will find our nation's history broken down into seven historical eras, from the Revolutionary War to post–World War II. For each era, an introductory essay provides historical context, with up to eight topics identified for each era. Each topic leads to a selection of items from the American Memory collections with study questions that also serve as a guide. Each item, in turn, is linked to the collection from which it came, which enables you to see the item in its entirety and also to search for other materials. This is a great way to identify appropriate material for independent activities and assignments without searching the collections directly.

Figure 3-3
The American Memory Timeline, a Learning Page feature, provides historical context to the eras represented in the collections and access to representative materials.

COLLECTION CONNECTIONS

Reviewing the Collection Connection documents on the Learning Page is another way to locate appropriate materials to use in your classroom. All collections have a summary page that guides you to special presentations within the collection and related collections, exhibits, and materials. This will help you get a sense of the content of the collection, and it provides fundamental search guidance. Figure 3-4 shows the Collection Connections page for Walt Whitman's notebooks. Some collections have a teaching resource page that highlights curriculum themes that occur within the collection with examples from the collection. Like the Timeline, clicking on the example will take you directly into the collection where you can

Figure 3-4

Collection Connection: Walt Whitman Notebooks. Through the Learning Page, the Collection Connection documents provide historical context and search tips for individual American Memory collections.

review that item in its entirety or search for more materials using some of the techniques described later in this chapter.

The Collection Connection index is arranged by collection title. Thus, you have to know the name of the collection you wish to review in this fashion. What is the quickest way to identify individual collections of possible interest? Try the Pathfinder indices, accessible through the Getting Started section of the Learning Page. This is a basic natural language, collection-level index. It is one of several tools you will use if you want to search the American Memory collections directly.

LESSON PLANS

You may be lucky enough to discover a teacher-created lesson plan that you can adapt for use in your classroom. You can use the lesson plan as is, adapt it to your needs, or scale it to a higher or lower performance level. Most, but not all lesson plans, were contributed by American Memory fellows who studied about primary sources with Library of Congress staff and curators. These lesson plans are carefully developed and classroom tested. Typically lessons provide direct links to individual items within the American Memory collections. Even if you don't use the lesson in its entirety, these lists of resources represent a huge amount of saved search time. See the Grapes of Wrath in this lesson plan (see figure 3-5) for a good example of teacher-created lessons on the Learning Page.

SEARCH THE LEARNING PAGE FOR MORE . . .

What if you don't quickly find materials to use in your classroom? You can try a quick search of the Learning Page by typing a word in the search box on the upper-right-hand corner of your computer screen. You may find other useful

Figure 3-5
Online Lesson: "Grapes of Wrath: Scrapbooks and Artifacts." This is one of the
many teacher-created lessons that appear on the Learning Page. You may use
these lessons "as is" or customize to your classroom needs.

materials. If you don't, you are on to your next adventure: Learning how to
search the American Memory collections.

SEARCHING THE COLLECTIONS

There are three basic ways to search the American Memory collections: across all
collections, across a group of collections, and by individual collection. The first
two options are identical, except that different collections are included in the
search. Perhaps the most useful way that collections can be easily grouped relates
to the type or format of the original material. When searching individual collections, you will note that search features may vary depending upon the type of collection, when it was digitized, or if it was digitized by one of the Ameritech
partner libraries.

For help getting started, consult "Finding Items in American Memory," accessible from the Learning Page and from the Search page for each collection.[1] While
there is a basic search formula that works reasonably well, to really uncover the
gems of wisdom contained within these collections, you will need to learn more
about the architecture of the system. If you are a teacher, this would be a good time
to get acquainted with your library media specialist, if you aren't already!

Searching Groups of Collections

To begin, go to the American Memory home page and select Search. This will
bring up the screen shown in figure 3-6. Unless you specify a cluster of collections

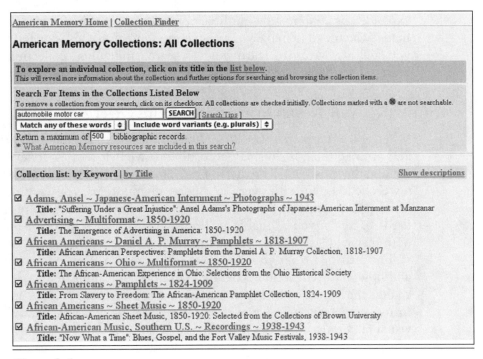

Figure 3-6
All Collections Search Page: Shown here is a keyword search across all American Memory collections.

by original format, words you enter in the search box will be searched against all collections. As you scroll down the list of collections, you will see a check box in front of each collection listed. You may *deselect* a collection from the search by clicking on the box.

On a cross-collection search, bibliographic information is searched; for those collections *without* rich bibliographic information, the full text is usually searched. This is an important consideration and one of the reasons that a cross-collection search should often be the first step, but not the last step, in finding appropriate materials. Note that graphics, background texts, and other interpretative materials within the collection are not searchable in this fashion. Note as well that a few collections are not searchable at all; these collections are identified with an "x." This does not mean that you cannot access these collections or materials, but it does mean that different techniques must be used. Access to non-searchable collections is discussed later in this chapter.

CONSTRUCTING YOUR SEARCH: BROAD OR NARROW?

Under the search box, notice two clickable options. These options set the search conditions, and they initially provide the widest possible search conditions: search for *any* of these words and search for *"word variants."* This means if you enter multiple words, the system will currently find any of those words and their plurals. Either option can be changed for a more precise search—search for *all* of those words or the *exact phrase.* Librarians will note that while the search can be expanded or contracted with these options, it cannot be focused to title or subject fields, which would make your search more precise. This is one of the reasons that you will also want to learn how to search individual collections, where many more search/browse techniques are available.

REVIEWING YOUR SEARCH: IS IT RELEVANT?

When you enter search words or phrases, the search engine will sort the responses and arrange them for display according to what it sees as "relevant." Items that contain the most "hits" are listed first. This is important because when you search a website like this with over 7.5 million digital items, you will inevitably get lots of false hits. Thus, with relevancy ranking, even if your search results return hundreds of items, you probably will not have to review all of them. You may also note that while the entire collection will be searched, currently only 500 records will be returned from your cross-collection search. Depending upon your search and how many collections you are searching, that limit may be too low. You can change the number of items returned on the search page. Note as well the option to use the "Gallery" display (see figure 3-7), which is a handy way to review visual materials.

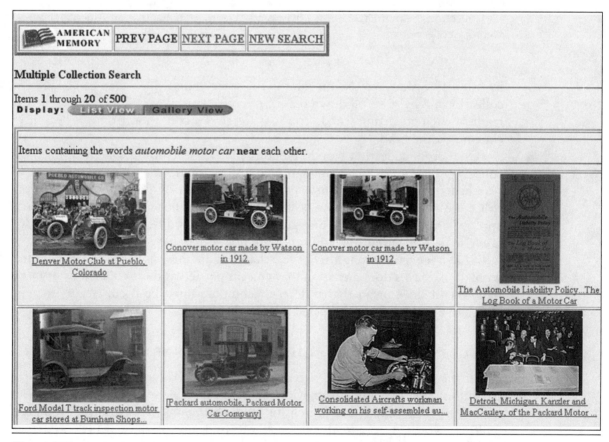

Figure 3-7
The Gallery-display option is a handy way to review search results, particularly with visual materials.

WHEN TO USE CROSS-COLLECTION SEARCHES

Cross-collection searches are useful as starting points, but often they are most helpful to identify individual collections that you want to search further. Search results are initially displayed in a list, showing first the collection from which each item comes and then the title of the item. This makes it very easy to determine which collections will be of most interest for further research. As noted earlier, the browse options available within specific collections are different and can be used to find additional materials.

As you gain more experience searching the collections, you will find a cross-collection search can be very effective when you are doing a presentation to teachers for whom the concept of primary sources is new. The optional Gallery display (figure 3-7) enables you to show thumbnail images of items side-by-side, making multiple formats more apparent. For example, if you search on the exact words, "Niagara Falls," within the first ten items you will find two early films, a panoramic map, a daguerreotype image, historic sheet music, a nineteenth-century advertisement, and a guidebook—ample testimony to the multimedia aspect of the American Memory collections.

Cross-collection searches by format are also very useful if, for example, you are looking for historical photographs to use in a visual literacy activity. If you wish to do this, limit your all-collections search to Photographs and Prints by clicking on that option in the right-hand side of your computer screen. Now, the list of collections that will be searched will include only those collections in which you will find photographs. What you have to keep in mind is that this broad category represents not only photograph collections, but document or multi-format collections *in which photographs appear.* This means your search may return items that are not photographs, which is initially confusing to novice searchers. You'll also find the gallery display helpful in pictorial collections because it is often difficult to express the message or "content" of an image in search words.

Searching Individual Collections

Once you are familiar with the scope of the American Memory collections through cross-collection searching, you will inevitably settle on a handful of favorite collections. Within individual collections, there will be search/browse options in addition to the keyword search that you used in cross collection searching. Once you open the home page of an individual collection, those additional options will become apparent. You know a book by its cover? This old cliché rings true here. To maximize your search, it is important that you get to know the collection by carefully perusing its home page.

GETTING TO KNOW THE COLLECTION

Often the home page of a collection is comprised of a collage with examples from the collection. (See figure 2-3.) Clicking on those representative images will take you to a page with bibliographic information and links to those items within the collection. Each home page will also have a description of its contents, sometimes with words or phrases highlighted and linked to the collection. Clicking on those links is like executing a "canned" search—a good way to get to materials considered important or representative of the collection. In some cases, these links provide access to items within the collection that are not easily found in a word search. Most collections also have special presentations prepared by curators or researchers that provide context for the collection and for individual items within the collection. Links to these presentations appear on the home page. Reviewing this type of contextual background material is important even before you begin to search.

If you scroll down to the bottom of the home page for each collection, you will see two categories of information: Understanding the Collection and Working with the Collection. Here you will find important background information about the collection, related resources—both print and online—and links to the Collection Connections feature of the Learning Page. These can also be important in getting to know the collection. Once you understand the nature of the collection, searching is going to be easier and more rewarding.

IDENTIFYING COLLECTIONS BY NAME

Perhaps you have previously identified a collection by name from a cross-collection search. If so, you can get to that collection by selecting Search or Collection Finder from the American Memory home page. The length of this list will depend upon whether you select all collections or collections by original format. The default arrangement of this list is by keyword. If you wish to arrange it alphabetically by title, click on the title option. Once you find the collection, click on the name to open it

If you haven't identified a collection by name, you can go to the Getting Started section of the Learning Page and find the How to Search segment. There you will find a link to Pathfinders. Here you will find five indices: Events, People, Places, Time, and Topic. Up until 2001, each American Memory collection that came online was indexed against this list of keywords, providing a quick way to find the names of collections that might be useful. Click on the collection name to open the collection. When using this search tool, however, keep in mind its lack of currency now affects its usefulness. Unless it is updated, if you rely solely on this tool, you will miss important resources.

SEARCH METHODS

Like a library catalog, American Memory collections can be searched using the cataloging information. This can be done in two ways: using keywords—words that appear some where in the catalog "card"—or by the specific kind of information—title, author, photographer, subject term, etc. This is called a bibliographic search because it searches the information that appears in the bibliographic record.

Like an online database, the full text of some American Memory collections can also be searched. This means that every word of the item itself—not just the description in the catalog card—is searchable. Sometimes the bibliographic search and the full-text search are combined in one step. Sometimes searching both ways requires two steps. This was not done to make your life complicated. Bibliographic and full-text searching were combined for collections in which it was too costly to assign subject terms to each item. Figure 3-8 shows a screen for searching bibliographic descriptions or full text.

SEARCH STRATEGIES

What do you want to find? Where will you find it? What words will you use to find it? When doing historical research, students sometimes find it difficult to think in the vocabulary of the time. You will find a number of tips about developing search vocabulary and search strategies from links on the search page of each collection. For example, if you were searching the collections for references to the black American experience, you would need to use words that were then used such as "colored, Negro, Negroes," and others. In a school environment, this exercise itself will generate a discussion that librarians and teachers will want to incorporate into the classroom lesson. Sometimes it is hard for teachers and students to come up with these alternative search words. Browsing the subject

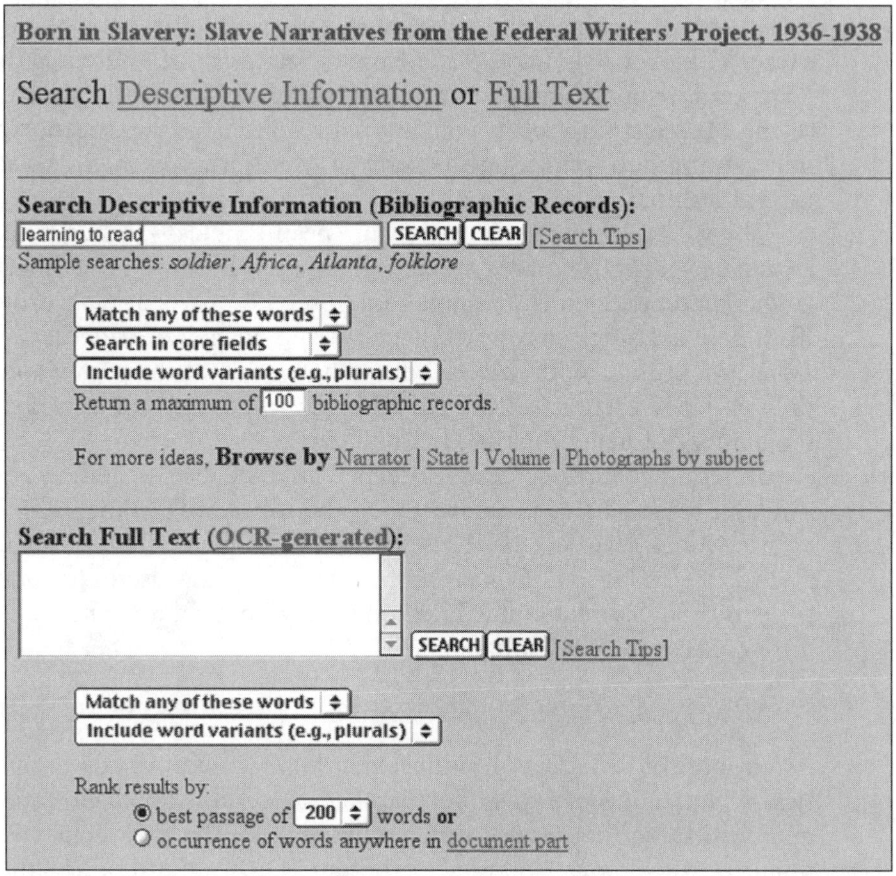

Born in Slavery: Slave Narratives from the Federal Writers' Project, 1936-1938

Search Descriptive Information or Full Text

Search Descriptive Information (Bibliographic Records):

learning to read   [SEARCH] [CLEAR] [Search Tips]
Sample searches: *soldier, Africa, Atlanta, folklore*

Match any of these words ⬍
Search in core fields ⬍
Include word variants (e.g., plurals) ⬍
Return a maximum of 100 bibliographic records.

For more ideas, **Browse by** Narrator | State | Volume | Photographs by subject

Search Full Text (OCR-generated):

[SEARCH] [CLEAR] [Search Tips]

Match any of these words ⬍
Include word variants (e.g., plurals) ⬍

Rank results by:
⦿ best passage of 200 ⬍ words **or**
○ occurrence of words anywhere in document part

Figure 3-8
Born in Slavery, Full-Text Search Page. In this collection, the full-text search is enhanced with a variety of options and the search is working on "dirty text"—text generated by optical character recognition (OCR).

lists in individual collections can be very helpful to teachers and students building new vocabulary for word searching. For example, browsing the subject terms from the *Selected Civil War Photographs* collection will reveal phrases like "horse artillery," "newspaper vendors," and "military cookery." There is also a synonym list online, which provides some examples and will get you thinking.[2]

What do you do if you find too much? Too little? Consult Tips for New Users, which is available online[3] (Accessible from the Learning Page/Getting Started/How to Search/Tools). One of the things you will soon discover is that searching is not an exact science. In fact, as you gain more experience, you will discover that it is an art that can be fine-tuned in a variety of ways.

BASIC BIBLIOGRAPHIC SEARCH

From each collection's home page, you will see a search option and one or two—sometimes more—browse options. The default search option in a single collection is the same as in a cross-collection search: search for *any* of these words and search for word "variants." Like cross-collection searching, both options can be changed for more precision, but in many of the collections that were digitized first, word searching cannot be limited to a specific field of information. For example, in *Touring Turn-of-the-Century America*, if you enter the search word "Missouri," you will find an image of the U.S.S. Missouri as well as a photograph of the Missouri Capitol in your search results. Had you been expecting to find only photographs depicting the state of Missouri, you might be surprised to see the battleship.

The way you find information in specific fields—author, title, creator, photographer, geographic area, place name, subject, etc.—is to browse that index. Unlike searching, which requires that you enter a word, with browsing you pick from a list. Using a browse list can result in a more focused, but somewhat awkward, search. With the current configuration of the search software, you can only pick one category at a time, and there is no indication in the browse list of the number of items contained in that category.

Different collections have different "browse" lists or indices. You will see the available indices listed prominently on the collection's home page. Some have one or two; some have several. These choices have generally been made by the curators for the collections. For example, a list of titles is useful for books, but less so for photographs; geographic location is very important for maps, less relevant for most collections of personal papers.

More Focused Bibliographic Search

In some of the later collections, an additional option of searching in the "core fields" was added, giving the searcher more control. The core fields include author, title, subject, and notes. Excluded from the core fields are identification numbers, such as call number or digital ID. In addition, specific fields can be selected for searching. These refined search features are especially important for collections in which the text is also fully searchable. Consult *Born in Slavery: Slave Narratives from the Federal Writers' Project, 1936–1938* for an example of this search enhancement.

Other collections have discrete segments that are handled differently to provide more flexibility. For example, *America from the Great Depression to World War II* contains both black-and-white photographs and color photographs. Because the images are cataloged differently, they have been arranged in separate collections with a bridge connecting the two segments as well as an option to search both segments together.

FULL-TEXT SEARCH

Most document collections provide both bibliographic searching as described above *and* full-text searching, meaning that each word in the text has been transcribed so that the search engine can locate it. But, there are a variety of ways in which this has been implemented.

In the collections first digitized, the text-search capability is basic, and perhaps sounds familiar by now: search for *any* of these words and search for "word variants." Similar to cross-collections searching, these settings can be changed for more precision. See *African American Perspectives: Pamphlets from the Daniel A. P. Murray Collection, 1818–1907* as an example. In this collection, bibliographic and full-text searching are two separate activities. It is usually easy enough to see search words in a bibliographic record, but when they appear in the text, they are much more difficult to find. When you choose a full-text search option, your search words are highlighted in the text view. You can move quickly through the document using the Best Match option. If you wish to see the look and the feel of this pamphlet, click on Page Image. You can also review the bibliographic information. This is simple and straightforward.

More Focused Full-Text Search

The text of other collections may require more complex searches, partially because the collections contain larger documents. For example, *American Ballroom Companion: Dance Instruction Manuals* has the same basic full-text search capability as the pamphlet collection, and likewise, bibliographic searching and full-text searching are two separate actions. In both cases, you need to scroll down on the screen to see the full-text search box. In this case, however, search results are displayed differently.

The dance manual collection is comprised of books, which have chapters. Thus, in this collection, a bibliographic search returns a list of book titles; a full-text search returns a list of book chapters. You will need to look carefully at the display prompts. If you are reviewing the search results for relevancy, you will want to examine the text and see where your search words appear. You'll be able to navigate through those pages section by section. If, however, you want to get a sense for the look and feel of this item, you will want to look at the page images. You'll be able to move back and forth through these modes of viewing by using the display prompts.

Other text collections have been enhanced with the core-field capability in the bibliographic search options, and the full-text search has also been further refined. *Born in Slavery: Slave Narratives from the Federal Writers' Project, 1936–1938* is a good example of a collection with enhanced search capabilities. In this collection, the text search has been enhanced with an additional feature that restricts words found to be within 200 words of each other, or in the same "document part." Generally, this would mean chapters, but it could also include other intellectual divisions. This technique controls the false hits that are inevitable with word searching—in the text or the bibliographic record.

Exceptions to the Rules

Some American Memory text collections are not fully searchable. Copyright restrictions or budget deficiencies are usually the culprits. For example, the manuscripts in *Thomas Jefferson Papers* were scanned into digital format from the microfilm collection held at the Library of Congress. This process produces the image of the page. For the text to be searchable, the words on the page must either be transcribed or converted through optical character recognition (OCR) into searchable text. OCR does not work well with manuscript collections. Because transcriptions of many of these documents already existed in published compilations, those that were not copyright restricted were used. This left some manuscripts without transcriptions, and, thus, not searchable. A note on the collection's search page explains which texts are searchable and which are not.

Century of Lawmaking for a New Nation: U.S. Congressional Documents and Debates, 1774–1875 provides full-text access to many, but not all, documents in the collection. Why this discrepancy? For the volume of material provided, transcribing all materials exceeded the available budget. As optical character recognition becomes more accurate, there is some thought that searchable text might be generated from the page images. For now, for those materials without searchable text, there are browse options. One unique feature of this collection is the ability to link from the *House Journal* or *Senate Journal* to items in related publications on the same date.

And, one text collection—*Poet at Work: Recovered Notebooks from the Thomas Biggs Harned Walt Whitman Collection*—is not searchable at all. Other than the Collection Connection feature on the Learning Page (see figure 3-4), the only access to this collection is through sequential browse indices. This is similar to flipping through the notebooks page by page. Through its Collection Connection, however, you will find direct links to Walt Whitman's handwritten notes, which record his thoughts about his literary work and his personal experiences during the Civil War.

INFORMATION LITERACY AND AMERICAN MEMORY

"Stop, stop!" I hear the teachers scream. "I don't want to find *everything;* I just want to find something that will work with my lesson." To be effective, school library media specialists must recognize this practical need but also help both teacher and students become more knowledgeable digital navigators. It is becoming an increasingly complex digital world. This will continue even more rapidly as more and more information becomes digital, either through conversion or by being "born digital." This is a fact of modern life. Today's students must know something about researching on the Web to be literate in the twenty-first century.

The American Memory collections are easy to search on one level, but a simple search may be insufficient to uncover the gems of knowledge and wisdom you can find nowhere else. One of the beauties of digital content is not only convenience, but access. Because of the range of full-text search techniques available, these collections can be accessed in ways that the collection designer may not have envisioned. Isn't this how new ideas develop? Isn't new knowledge forged through thinking, reading, writing, designing, building, and using old things in new ways?

Understanding the intricacies of search protocol, however, is not what teachers are trained to do. Librarians are. Recognizing the need for information, knowing how to find it, and then making sense of it are basic information-literacy skills—skills every school librarian learned in library school. Librarians can and should be working with teachers to identify potential resources that may not be known to exist. (These are the hardest to find!)

Yet, the librarian can only do this if he or she is considered an essential part of the instructional team, and this doesn't necessarily happen without a lot of hard work. Teachers often go it alone; they are used to being "in charge" in their classrooms. And, some librarians get so consumed with the technicalities of running a library that they don't market their skills in a proactive way. Here is the perfect opportunity! If you are a teacher, team up with your school library media specialist to find more materials of interest than you can quickly find via pre-established links on the Learning Page. If you are a librarian, go find a teacher— preferably a history, social studies or even a language arts teacher—and showcase the American Memory collections. Soon you will have created a "buzz" in the building and the library may become a very busy place, if it isn't already. You'll read more about this in chapter 5.

Proactive librarians consider themselves teachers. *Information Power*, a joint publication of the American Association of School Librarians (AASL) and the Association for Educational Communications and Technology (AECT), describes a librarian as a teacher of students, an instructional partner, an information specialist, and a program administrator.[4] As a *teacher*, the librarian develops information-literacy skills in the learning community. As an *instructional partner*, the librarian works collaboratively with other staff in designing authentic learning tasks to exercise principles of information literacy. As an *information specialist*, the librarian provides leadership in information and technology. As a *program administrator*, the librarian provides leadership, vision, and creativity to a library media program, making it responsive to its users' needs. To mine the American Memory collections for connections across the curriculum for the entire school, the proactive school librarian will wear all four of these hats.

Librarians are not arbitrators of information literacy; they are champions. Thus, the AASL in cooperation with AECT has published nine "Information Literacy Standards for Student Learning." These are published as a chapter in *Information Power*, and they are also available as a separate publication from AASL. The standards are arranged in three categories. Most of us recognize that students should know how to identify a need for information, how to analyze it, and how to use it. But, we sometimes overlook the second category: how important it is to develop independent learners—students who can use these research skills to pursue their own personal interests, who can be appreciative of others' efforts, and who recognize excellence. The third category relates social responsibility in a democratic society, echoing the sentiments of the Librarian of Congress, that by making its digital resources freely accessible, the Library of Congress supports a knowledgeable citizenry.

Lofty goals such as these can best be translated into action by teachers and librarians working collaboratively on a student activity, lesson, or project. You'll be integrating information-literacy standards with content standards and be off on a learning adventure that may change your practice of teaching.

NOTES

1. "Finding Items in American Memory" [online], available from http://memory.loc.gov/ammem/ndlpedu/orientation/find.html.

2. "Synonym List" [online], available from http://memory.loc.gov/ammem/ndlpedu/start/synonym.html.

3. "Tips for New Users" [online], available from http://memory.loc.gov/ammem/searchtp/amindex.html#sim.

4. American Association of School Librarians (AASL) and Association for Educational Communications and Technology (AECT), *Information Power: Building Partnerships for Learning* (Chicago: ALA, 1998).

CHAPTER FOUR

Strategies for Teaching History

STANLEE BRIMBERG

Let's say that your state or district has done a plausible job in articulating social studies goals. Until now, you've lived with the materials and the methodologies you have available to support those goals. Now, you realize that you have access to a virtually limitless number of online documents and images, films, and audio. Maybe you've been encouraged, or even mandated, to get into them, to teach students to think and work like historians. In a way, you are the educational equivalent of the wagoner who traveled on the Oregon Trail to get to San Francisco in 1849 when news of the discovery of gold reached the East. Like that adventurer, you are aware of the prospect of riches beyond what you might ever have imagined; at the same time, you never know if and when that winter storm will come, or that black bear will rampage through your campsite. You sense the forces you are dealing with are, well . . . big.

A list of important questions and concerns about primary sources begins to emerge: How many documents? Which ones? How often should I use them? What happens if most of the students don't understand the document or can't make any sense of the image? Where do I find the time and energy to create curriculum and at the same time do justice to my job as a teacher of children? Seven million or more items on American Memory? It may as well be seven hundred million! How am I going to deal with this? These are concerns that would lead many an intrepid adventurer to turn the wagon around and go back to Philadelphia.

This chapter provides a map, a handbook, and guidance. It doesn't prescribe where you should go or what you should experience; rather it suggests ways to deal with the challenges the journey presents.

Stanlee Brimberg is a teacher in New York City.

YOUR JOURNEY WITH PRIMARY SOURCES

Establishing Perspective

If you were a photojournalist covering an important event, you would need a variety of shots, long shots to establish a sense of the whole, the setting, and then you would want a variety of medium shots and close-ups so that your audience could see the actions and responses of groups of people and individuals. Likewise, when you study an event or an era, students need to walk away with the long view and the close-ups. So, maybe it's useful to think about teaching history by extending the metaphor: The long, wide-angle views may be provided by your textbook, the introductory comments you make, or summaries of periods or events that others have prepared. The medium shots, and in particular the close-ups, will come from the primary-source documents and images.

Before we had access to primary sources, we had to rely on someone else's long view. But even when we use the actual words that people said and images of places and events, the stories we tell can never be purely objective. Just as the film-maker makes decisions about what will be in the frame, now teachers, rather than textbook editors, become the mediators of historical content. Choices about how to spend time and resources determine to a large extent the stories students will know and remember. As educators, we have to be mindful of striking a balance.

It's temping to rely too much on the close-ups. But the resulting *understandings*, while well-intended, may resemble the perceptions that the six blind men had of the elephant in the old Indian fable, each man characterized the entire animal by the part he himself touched.[1] Students need the long view so that they can make sense of the close-ups. They need to leave with a sense of the story. The documents and images provide essential pieces, but they are not the story.

History is made up of *many* stories. Your job as the teacher and curriculum planner is to decide what should be included and how deep to go. Your task is to help children understand and identify the points of view, to see patterns, and to ask interesting questions. You need to create a rhythm in your class so that students understand that they will sometimes move quickly through events and at other times they will consider one moment very carefully. Unless you learn to think like a curriculum planner, even the excellent uses of the resources described later in this book will be recipes you follow literally instead of models that will inspire you to tinker and tailor materials for your students.

Curriculum Planner or Travel Agent?

Planning a study, or even one activity in a large curriculum, is very much like planning a family vacation. If you went to a travel agency, you would most likely be asked to consider these questions: Where do you want to go? How much time do you have? How much money do you want to spend? How will you travel? What will you want to do? Where will you want to stay? Will there be activities that are appropriate for the whole family? What will each of the family members need in order to take advantage of this vacation? After the trip is over, will you allow us to ask you how it went?

These questions all have counterparts in curriculum planning: What is the content? How much class time can you spend on it? What resources are available to you? What kinds of activities and what methods shall you use to teach the content? Who are your students? How can you accommodate their different needs in the course of this unit? How will you know what has been learned? The first question is a big and important one.

What Is the Content?

To many people, content means information. For the purposes of this book, we'll take a broader view. Content is any of the stuff that students will encounter in the course of studying the material. Included in the idea of content are three things: *concepts*, *information*, and *skills*. To make good decisions about curriculum, you need to understand something about all three aspects of content.

Concepts

All historical studies—all studies of any kind—have underlying concepts. Concepts are the cubbies that hold information. They help us organize things so each piece of data is not discrete. Some people call them big ideas, others call them understandings. Some people state them as a word or phrase, like "transportation" or "consequences of technology." Others state concepts as sentences:

> History is not one story, but many stories that may interweave.

The point of a concept, in contrast to an item of information, is that it isn't tied to a particular instance. It's transferable to other settings. Here is an item of information:

> The American Revolution began in Lexington, Massachusetts, in April 1775. It's specific. It's about one event. Here are two related concepts under which that piece of information might be filed:

> People respond to conflict in many ways.

> When the governed are dissatisfied with their government, one alternative has been to rebel in the hope of bringing about a sudden, revolutionary change.

These concepts apply throughout history—not only in America, but also in China, Russia, and in other places in Asia, Africa, and South America. Concepts relate the information to a bigger idea.

IDENTIFYING CONCEPTS

There are probably a hundred or so concepts that are important in social studies (historical, political, economic, geographical, etc.). As teachers who are creating curricular activities, how do we decide which concepts should underlie our activities? Working with seventh graders, I've converged on fewer than a dozen concepts that seem so pervasive, both in terms of history and self-awareness, that I feel are essential to my curriculum. They are as follows:

History is not one story, but many stories, some of which interweave.

History isn't only about power, although people who have steered or redirected the lives of groups of others have made history.

Sometimes an individual who makes history may be powerful in his or her own time, but sometimes he or she lives an ordinary life.

Often, ordinary people are affected by historical events that, at first, may seem to have nothing to do with them.

When we study history, it's important to develop an understanding of the context of the people we are studying. We have to know how they expressed themselves, what certain words meant to them, how they got their needs met, what they cared about and believed in, what their material culture was, what the level of technology was, what they wore, what they read, what music they listened to, and so on.

Historical events often have many causes and many effects.

Events that happened long ago may have a profound effect on our lives today.

Geography is destiny. The way that people live and what they value are almost always affected by their geography. Alternatively, people affect their geography (by building a canal, by damming a river, by building a city, by polluting the air, etc.).

Economics concerns the way a group of people creates and distributes wealth.

Democracy in America, the acquisition of liberty and civil rights, has been a process that has been unfolding and expanding from the minute the Constitution was ratified to the present. The desire for freedom and civil rights is a historical universal. All rational people want to be free.

ARTICULATING CONCEPTS

Some of the concepts that I have identified might resonate with you. But state or district curricular frameworks and standards, school expectations, student populations and values, attitudes, and beliefs all differ. For that reason, you will want to have your own list, and it may be different from mine. Try to articulate the concepts yourself. What are the understandings that underlie the information? Are there patterns that may be seen elsewhere? What lessons may be learned about people? Is there a moral to the story?

Where do you find concepts? First, look at your local social studies curriculum or the social studies standards. Then, check with lists of concepts in the teacher's edition of your textbook. Don't forget to think about concepts that have already been part of your study. Examine your own mind. What are the lessons of history you wish to pass on to your students?

Try hard not to get overwhelmed by all the concepts that could apply. Less is more. Keep your conceptual goals modest and look for materials and activities that will enable students to encounter and reencounter the same few concepts in different places. You want to hear students saying things like, "Oh, I get it, this is just like when . . . ." That introduction is your way of assessing that conceptual thinking is at work.

Information

This is the part that traditionally is considered to be historical content. It's names and dates, battles and outcomes, treaties, declarations and laws, elections, conquests, great disasters, and so on. It's not the concept of a disaster, but the instance—the Great Chicago Fire. It is not the understanding of what war is, but World War II. It's the specific example.

You don't need dozens of primary sources to shotgun an era. You may end up looking for just one or two that present the opportunity to go from informational understanding to conceptual understanding. An example of this follows later in this chapter, and more examples appear in subsequent chapters of this book.

CATEGORIES OF INFORMATION

The materials you'll encounter in American Memory and other primary-source websites will often fall into one of three categories of information: an official document; personal commentary about an event; and documents and images representative of an era, but not tied to a specific event.

In the first category, you will find important historical documents, like the U.S. Constitution, the Declaration of Independence, or the lyrics to the "Star-Spangled Banner" (see figure 4-1 for the first printed copy of the "Star-Spangled Banner"). This kind of information is important because part of what we want students to do is learn to live in a democracy. This requires knowledge of basic history. The gradual construction of historical understanding comprises not only a framework (the concepts), but documents such as these form the bricks, windows, doors, and rooms (the information).

The second category would include a document or image that refers to, discusses, or is in some way is obviously affected by an important historical event, such as the passages from the *George Washington Papers* wherein he describes his encounter with the French at Fort Duquesne. This kind of document is important because students need to encounter and reencounter the idea that historical events have consequences for both famous and ordinary people and because students need to see that not everyone feels the same way about an important event.

The third category groups interesting or stimulating documents and images representing a period in history, but with no clear or obvious connection to an important historical event. The value of this kind of information has to do with the student's need to have a mental picture of the time about which he or she is learning. From the narratives of ordinary people such as those found in the American Memory collection, *American Life Histories, 1936–1940* and the images from a collection like *Touring Turn-of-the-Century America, 1880–1920*, students will develop of sense of what things looked and felt like. Students need to see a "mental movie." These materials help them construct the set and see the furniture and costumes—to get a sense of the texture of a place.

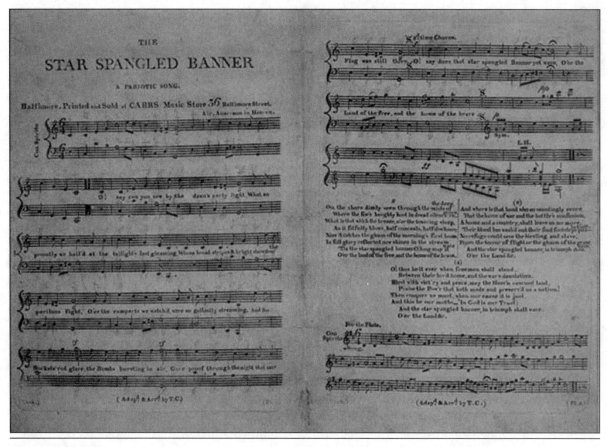

Figure 4-1
Shown here is the first printed copy of the "Star Spangled Banner" combining both words and music. From the online exhibition *American Treasures of the Library of Congress*.

Skills

Students need certain skills to make sense of the information we present in order to connect the information—the instance—to the concept. To do this, they will practice and extend old skills and, presumably, learn new ones. Since groups of students come to you with a wide range of skills, it is vital that you think through how you're going to bring everyone along.

In general, there are two kinds of skills that apply to documents and images: *verbal literacy*, that is, the ability to make meaning from written words, and *visual (or auditory) literacy*, in which we get information from images (or sounds). They are articulated here in these social studies standards for grades 6–8:

1. Knows the defining characteristics of a variety of informational texts (e.g., textbooks; biographical sketches; letters; diaries; directions; procedures; magazines; essays; primary source historical documents; editorials; news stories; periodicals; bus routes; catalogs; technical directions; consumer, workplace, and public documents).

2. Knows different types of primary and secondary sources and the motives, interests, and bias expressed in them (e.g., eyewitness accounts, letters, diaries, artifacts, photos, magazine articles, newspaper accounts, hearsay).[2]

To a greater extent, the concepts and information may be prescribed. While it's important to choose information and concepts that are relevant to the lives of the students, they might still understand content even if the material seems foreign or unfamiliar to them. With primary sources such as those available from the Library of Congress, teachers have to be much more careful to make a match between resources and students for a very obvious reason: if students can't make sense of the material, we are wasting their time and energy and our own. So it's important to identify the common problems students have when they encounter primary source documents and to suggest strategies to overcome them.

BASIC LITERACY

The verbal skills necessary to make sense of primary source documents all involve reading—from basic skills like decoding to higher-order thinking skills like getting the main idea, making inferences, recognizing assumptions, and the like.

Many important documents may be difficult for students to comprehend simply because they were written in a time when people used different words, different idioms, and different sentence lengths from what we do now. Consider the first sentence of the Gettysburg Address:

> Four score and seven years ago, our fathers brought forth on this continent a new nation, conceived in liberty and dedicated to the proposition that all men are created equal.

Think about contemporary English-language conventions. Then, think about your students. Try to imagine where in the sentence their comprehension might break down to the point where they can't make sense of it. Next, think about what they have to know how to do to get from the original passage to something like this:

Eighty-seven years ago (1863, when the speech was delivered, minus 4 × 20 plus 7, or 87: That's 1776!) a group of men Lincoln is calling "our fathers" (because they *fathered* our country, not because they were literally relatives) designed a plan for the new country. Their plan was based largely on the idea that people want freedom and are equal to each other. "Okay, I get it," nods the student.

So far this is a comprehension activity. We can get as fancy and creative as we like in thinking of ways to celebrate an important document, but unless our students can take it (or part of it), read it, and then understand it and use it, all of the posters, murals, and role plays are just window dressing. Figure 4-2 lists some typical difficulties that students have with primary-source text and some suggestions about how to deal with them.

Mediate the content; don't be steamrolled by it. By this I mean, examine your teaching objectives first rather than let the content dictate the activity. For example, depending on your class, your time, your energy, and your curriculum, you might have your class memorize the Gettysburg Address and make a two-

Difficulties	*Suggested Solutions*
The passage is written in period syntax, with many clauses or a lot of unfamiliar language. The handwriting or typeface may have characters that are unfamiliar.	1. Make and distribute a key that defines difficult vocabulary or that explains unfamiliar idioms or characters. If you know how to edit html docs, download the passage and make hyperlinks to definitions and explanations. 2. Take one or more sample documents and translate them together as you might if the passage were written in another language. Teach students to divide sentences into what they think are the chunks of meaning in them, to paraphrase each, and to put them back together. You might have students take a few sentences and "re-line" them as a poem. Divide and conquer.
The document is very long.	1. Don't use the whole document. Find the part(s) you consider essential and present only those. Offer extra credit to those students who volunteer to read the whole document. 2. Do sections of the document on different days. 3. Divide the document into parts and assign small groups to interpret each part. Take turns reading the pieces of the document in order and discuss the meaning of the whole.
The document contains language that is considered offensive today or discusses a subject that is disturbing.	1. Don't let this go. Prepare the kids before they examine the document by discussing the literal meaning of the words or phrases, what they meant at that time, and what they mean now. 2. Make it clear that you aren't endorsing the use of that language. Allow the students to discuss their own discomfort. 3. If language or a topic seems to be very uncomfortable for your students, decide whether you really need to use that document.

Figure 4-2
Tips for helping students understand primary-source text.

hour video about it; or, you might spend two periods studying just the last line and then move on.

VISUAL LITERACY

Pictures are, very obviously, a qualitatively different medium from text. And, since our students look at images almost constantly, many of them have tremendous expertise in interpreting them. But, we need to teach them to examine images with a critical eye.

When we use images to teach history, we need to establish a frame of reference, a context for the images, just as we do for text. The obvious place to start is by asking students what they see. There is a gestalt that viewers get from pictures that they don't get from text, but students need to learn how to codify this experience.

When I begin a piece of fiction with a class, I usually do a close reading of the first two pages and discuss the passage by asking the class what we are told literally and what we may infer from what we are told. I think it's important to do the same thing with pictures. A sod house or a barefoot child, for example, might look like poverty to our students, but it may not imply abject poverty in its historical context. Much of the time, the reason I want students to look at images is to develop that sense of historical context—that there were no Jeeps or tanks at the Battle of Bull Run, that the oven in the cabin of a slave was not made by GE. I want students to notice whether clothing was manufactured or homemade, how people wore their hair and used adornments.

So when I ask my students to do a close observation of a picture, often as a small group activity, I have them make their notes in two columns: "What I See" and "What I Think It Means."

There are three categories of observations: *the setting*; *the people*; and *the choices* made by the artist, photographer, or filmmaker. The first two are more literal, and the third more inferential. The third category is also more subtle, but with a little coaching, students become quite adept at thinking about it: Why did the person who made the picture show what he or she showed? What is left out? What seems candid? What seems staged? What message is the maker of the image trying to give us?

Figure 4-3 is a photograph I've used for several years in a Civil War study.[3] This photograph comes from the *Selected Civil War Photographs, 1861–1865*, American Memory collection. The

Figure 4-3
Two officers—one Union, the other Confederate—sit side by side. From *Selected Civil War Photographs, 1861–1865*, American Memory collection.

man on the right is Col. George Armstrong Custer, fighting for the Union. The man on the left is a Confederate prisoner named James B. Washington. I know that from the bibliographic information, which I don't share with the students at this point.

So, after making literal observations about the setting and the people, what might be learned from it? I ask my students to try to hypothesize about the circumstances that would lead a Union officer to be sitting on a box next to a Confederate officer, whom we are told is a prisoner. The students' responses vary:

> "Custer was proud that he captured an officer and was showing off."

> "He was a sadist, so he posed his prisoner with him, the way a cat toys with a mouse."

At last, I tell them about the bibliographic information I found in a stereoscope of the same photograph in another American Memory collection, *Civil War Treasures from the New-York Historical Society*.[4] It turns out the two men were classmates at West Point. Friends, I infer.

Now, I will ask them, what do you think? We talk some more. I am hoping to get students to consider something about the nature of conflict. What's the difference between having a conflict between two groups and a conflict within a group? Students will very naturally bring their own experiences of conflicts to a discussion about this. Ultimately, that's what we want. That is the whole point: we want students to recognize that everyday human forces and emotions play out in history; that the stories they learn about in history are like the stories they experience in their lives. And, that each can inform the other over an entire lifetime.

MANAGING STUDENT LEARNING

A lot of each student's education has to do with the gradual development of a map—a jigsaw puzzle that represents the learner's worldview. The more pieces that are placed on the puzzle, the more sense it makes. As new pieces are added, the student revises his or her view of things: How does this puzzle look *now*? Where does this new piece belong? If I put this piece in the right place, what might I see that I couldn't see before? How does this help me understand the bigger picture?

What do your students bring to the table when they are learning history? How does this affect what materials you choose and how you use them? Just as they come with a variety of skills, groups of children come to you with a range of prior knowledge. The children who have five hundred pieces of the puzzle filled in before the study begins will have an easier time with new content than children who have only five. The children in the latter group will likely need more skill development *and* more knowledge.

It's a challenge for the child with little prior knowledge to catch up. My experience is that the answer is not to barrage a child with facts to try to make up for lost time. Yet, at the same time, it's difficult for learners to really make sense of content that they can't connect to things they already know. How do we bring those students in?

It's all about the introduction to the activity and the resources. First, everyone likes to know what's coming. People are annoyed when they are blindsided. They are happier with a map. Next, having background information in advance of dealing with a primary source is like reading the synopsis of the libretto in the program notes before you see the opera. It enables you to whisper gleefully to your friend, "Oh, this is when *she* goes into the crypt *with* him because she *loves* him!" There is an aspect of any good educational experience that feels like solving a riddle, and there is tremendous gratification and power in simply "getting it." If you present a few consecutive activities in which your students are cracking the code and getting it, many will start to find the work pleasurable. They'll tell you that you make history fun, but what they mean is that you've learned how to pose appropriate riddles that feel good to solve. The satisfaction factor should not be underrated as motivation.

The Fine Art of Introductions

To see some good examples of how easily comprehensive activity setups may be constructed, look at the introductions to the documents in Diane Ravitch's excellent book *The American Reader: Words That Moved a Nation*. Those introductions are often shorter than a page in length and they set the stage beautifully. Here's how Ravitch introduces the lyrics of a popular pre-Revolutionary War tune:

> The tune and some stanzas of "Yankee Doodle" were familiar in the British colonies long before the Revolution. Even before the 1770's, British troops said "Yankee Doodle" to express derision for the colonists; early versions of the lyrics mocked the courage of the colonials and their rude dress and manners. "Yankee" was a pejorative term for a New England "bumpkin," and "doodle" was a simpleton or foolish fellow. However, during the Revolution the American troops adopted "Yankee Doodle" as their own song, a statement of pride in their simple, homespun dress and lack of affectation. There are many different versions of the lyrics. Over the years, the song has served as an unofficial anthem and favorite nursery song.[5]

The irony of the entire original lyric, which may be found in several incarnations in the *America Singing* American Memory collection, might be too subtle to understand without framing it in this way, especially since some of the slang a "bumpkin" might have used is long gone from present-day Yankee patois (see figure 4-4). With this introduction, however, children might be helped along to see that this is the story of a country fellow visiting a Revolutionary War encampment, who becomes overwhelmed and confused by what he sees. For example, when he observes Washington with a crowd of people around his horse, he reports that he's heard the "captain" has become so "tarnal proud" that he won't ride anywhere unless his horse is surrounded by people.

We might spend a class period trying to understand the stanzas in that light and then ask students why the Americans might have adopted a lyric that was so clearly critical of them. Then, we might think of present-day examples wherein

Figure 4-4
A song sheet pokes fun at the "yanke doodle" colonists.
From *America Singing: Nineteenth-Century Song Sheets*,
American Memory collection.

Classroom Culture

Much of the success you have with diverse materials and diverse children will have to do with how you deal with that diversity—the culture of your class. Here are some important questions related to differences and some suggestions:

terms that were made up to insult a group of people have been co-opted by the intended victims and used as a badge of pride or defiance.[6]

Depending on the kind of learners you're working with, the introduction can be written or discussed. Students who are more knowledgeable can help provide the context for those who need it in a "go-around" in which you take notes on a chart. You might write a background passage and some questions about it for homework the night before you present the document or image.

Encountering the same material in different ways, a kind of positive *redundancy* is another important technique we can use to motivate students. It's human nature to like things you know about and to be cool to things about which you know little. So coming at the same or related information in different ways is a method by which students slowly but surely begin to develop the expertise they need to have affection for a topic. For example, over the course of our Civil War unit, we read speeches by Frederick Douglass, who is depicted in an 1881 lithograph titled "Heroes of the Colored Race" (figure 4-5). We also read a chapter about him in Joy Hakim's book *War, Terrible War*, letters and articles about him from other sources, and passages from his autobiography. By the time he shows up in a cameo role in the dinner party scene in the movie *Glory*, my students are often quite excited at their recognition of Douglass. By this time, any subsequent information about Douglass has something to stick to.[7]

Figure 4-5
A lithograph depicting Frederick Douglass (center) with Blanche K. Bruce and Hiram Revels, both U.S. senators during the reconstruction years. From the American Memory collection, *African American Odyssey.*

How can you acknowledge that people bring different knowledge and skills to the table? If you set a tone in the class that takes that bull by the horns, students follow along with it easily. Project the idea that people deserve respect not because of what they know, but because they are people. Encourage students to listen respectfully and deeply by modeling it. Let students know what's correct and incorrect, but compliment plausible guesses and, especially, good, interesting questions, which are often as important as correct answers.

How can you plan activities that provide different levels of access and a range of challenges so that no one is bored on the one hand or frustrated on the other? One possible solution is to put together an activity that first leads students to a basic, or literal, understanding of the material. Then, make a second level of challenge that requires students to use that basic understanding to do or make something. Allow time or provide a vehicle through which students can ask further questions (a follow-up small group discussion, a journal entry). Vary the height of the bar for different students. Keep it high, but not insuperable, for all of them. Decide which parts of an activity are mandatory and which are voluntary.

What should be the body of knowledge that you can reasonably expect all your students to master? This really depends on your population. To me, developing expertise in a few things is better than having students memorize a lot of forgettable facts about a lot of things, and my own preference between conceptual and factual knowledge is the former. So I would want all my students to be able to use some correct historical (and personal) information to demonstrate their understanding of all the concepts we learn, but students with more mature worldviews will usually be able to do that using more information in more sophisticated ways.

WHAT HAVE STUDENTS LEARNED?

Perhaps it makes sense to think once again about that Indian fable, the blind men and the elephant. If each ends his assessment of the elephant with his first interview, his interpretation of what an elephant is would be in error, not because his perception is incorrect, but because it is incomplete. While some instruments of assessment are more or less formal, more or less modern, and more or less in vogue, I feel most comfortable when I use many of them in combination. The more times and ways we observe the whole elephant, the more likely we are to converge on an accurate assessment of what has been learned.

The most obvious, but often overlooked and underrated, method of assessment is to pay attention to how well students do each day, and to make mental and physical notes of how they interact with the materials. I keep a regular old-fashioned composition notebook with tabs on the margin so that each student has two pages. Over the course of the year, I write down some of the things each child says and does. Patterns invariably emerge.

Observational Framework

SOME QUESTIONS WHEN USING TEXT:

Does the student decode with some fluency, self-correct, and read with some expression that leads me to believe the student is making sense of the text?

Does the student have reading vocabulary waiting so that she or he can *pronounce* the word once it is sort of decoded?

Can the student tell which parts of the passage are difficult?

Does the student have comprehension strategies so that she or he can make meaning out of a passage even if parts are difficult? Is the interpretation logical?

Can the student paraphrase the passage?

Can the student relate the meaning of the passage to some bigger topic under consideration?

IF THE MATERIAL IS GRAPHIC, HERE ARE SOME QUESTIONS TO CONSIDER:

Can the student make literal observations of a picture and tell the difference between making observations and inferences?

Can the student make reasonable guesses about the material culture by looking at things like dress, adornments, building materials, and technology?

Can the student figure out why the artist or photographer framed what she or he did?

Can the student speculate about any visual evidence that the picture was posed or set up? What is that evidence?

Can the student speculate about whether the artist or photographer had a point of view and what that might be?

If the picture has a narrative element, can the student tell what the story might be?

Assessment Models

There are principally three modes in which students work with materials: as a whole class considering and discussing something together, in smaller groups of two to six students, and as individuals. It's important to assess the skills needed in each of these situations. There are entire books written about how these arrangements affect learning, but, in general, you might want to consider looking at these skills:

WHOLE CLASS OR LARGE-GROUP SKILLS ASSESSMENT

Can the student attend? For how long? If not, what is he or she doing?

What is the nature of the participation in a large group? That is, is the student a speculator of new ideas, a synthesizer of what others say, a summarizer?

Is the student taking advantage of the collective knowledge of the group? How do you know?

Can the student take good, useful notes? How can you tell?

SMALL-GROUP SKILLS ASSESSMENT

Can the student cooperate? Compromise? Make decisions?

How does the student divide the work?

How does that student demonstrate ownership of his or her part of the task?

What is the nature of the communication among group members?

INDIVIDUAL SKILLS ASSESSMENT

Has the student had enough practice with the skills learned in groups to do the work alone?

How does the student organize the task?

What strategies does the student use to proceed?

What, if anything, stops the student from completing the task well?

For each of these three basic configurations, we can design tasks. The last one, working individually, is probably most traditional: we can give a test and observe the student's performance. While I have no problem with written tests, per se, I like to remember that each type of question (matching, multiple choice, fill-in, essay, etc.) has its own set of skills that is related to the content but not dependent on it. First, we have to be careful to make sure that the student has those test-taking skills so that we don't confuse poor testing skills with a lack of mastery of the materials.

Additional assessment methodologies that are equally telling might involve more engaging activities. For example, students can use the primary sources as raw materials for presentations such as a story in the first person written and role-played by a student, a drama or debate played out in class, or in a scrapbook in which a student or a group of students use the text and images studied as inspiration.

CONNECTING OLD DOCUMENTS AND YOUNG PEOPLE

Many of the activities in this book call for students to use documents and images in combination with each other. Others call for students to use materials for making and doing things that seem bigger and more ambitious than what I've described in this chapter. All are engaging, educational activities that encourage historical thinking and creativity. In a sense, I feel that I am the one whose role it is to remind you, as you are running outside to play, to look both ways before you cross the street; to take your galoshes in case of rain; to keep in mind that someone—*you*—has to be the tether so that important, clear, useful connections may be made between wonderful old documents and wonderful young people.

NOTES

1. Using the poem "The Blind Men and the Elephant" by John Godfrey Saxe is an excellent way to get across to students the importance of perspective and the power of point of view. Use an Internet search engine to find a copy of the poem online. Search on "The Blind Men and the Elephant."

2. From McREL Searchable Database of Standards, available from http://www.mcrel.org/standards-benchmarks/.

3. Search on the keywords "Custer Confederate prisoner" to find this and other images in *Selected Civil War Photographs, 1861–1865* [online], available from http://memory.loc.gov/ammem/cwphtml/cwphome.html.

4. Search on the keywords "Custer Confederate prisoner" to find bibliographic information linking the two men to West Point in *Civil War Treasures from the New-York Historical Society* [online], available from http://memory.loc.gov/ammem/ndlpcoop/nhihtml/cwnyhshome.html.

5. Diane Ravitch, ed., *The American Reader: Words That Moved a Nation* (New York: HarperCollins, 1990), 11.

6. Search on the words "Yankee Doodle" to find this and other images in *America Singing: Nineteenth-Century Song Sheets* [online], available from http://memory.loc.gov/ammem/amsshtml/amsshome.html.

7. Search on the phrase "Frederick Douglass" in *African American Odyssey* [online], available from http://memory.loc.gov/ammem/aaohtml/exhibit/aointro.html.

CHAPTER FIVE

It's Elementary!

GAIL PETRI

I am often asked incredulously how sophisticated primary sources—*old* documents, pictures, manuscripts and the like—can be used to engage *young* children in learning. The skeptics will scoff: "Historical materials are boring! The text is too long! The vocabulary is difficult! The print is too small!" How can teachers use these materials in *elementary* school?

The real answer to that question lies in the questions generated and the stories told. My colleague Doris Waud often uses this 1863 photograph of a Gettysburg battlefield to begin a fifth-grade unit on the Civil War (figure 5-1).[1] Imagine her students' amazement when they look beyond the photograph to the caption and discover that the man in the photograph is actually her husband's great-grandfather, then an artist at *Harper's Weekly*! Can you imagine the barrage of questions that then follow?

Just as it does for adults, a real-life poignant image brings history alive for elementary school students and provides a springboard to learning and inquiry. Photographs, prints, and movies provide vivid *image pictures*. Authentic documents like newspapers, journals, advertisements, diaries, and letters create vivid *word pictures*. Songs, sounds, and oral histories provide *auditory pictures* to add depth and understanding to image and print documents. Using primary sources such as these help students connect the past to the present.

As a library media specialist at Fyle Elementary School in Rochester, New York, I provide teachers with materials to help them teach the required curriculum. Exposing students and teachers to primary resources, collaborating with many creative teachers on primary-source projects, and spreading the word about

---

Gail Petri is a library media specialist in Rochester, New York.

Figure 5-1
Alfred Waud, *Harper's Weekly* artist and
great-grandfather of the author's colleague,
seen sketching the Gettysburg battlefield.
From *Selected Civil War Photographs,
1861–1865,* American Memory collection.

primary sources to the broader educational community have been my goals. This chapter outlines some of the strategies, activities, and projects that I have found to be successful in integrating primary resources across the elementary school curriculum.

GETTING STARTED WITH PRIMARY SOURCES

For me, it all started at the Library of Congress. My experience as a Library of Congress American Memory Fellow in the summer of 2000 changed my teaching methods. I was amazed to discover photographs, documents, audio files, and movies—millions of online resources—all available with a simple click of a mouse. I was positive that these remarkable primary sources could be used to excite elementary school children about history. I was convinced that they could be used to encourage them to think like historians. But how could I help teachers learn about what was available? Were the necessary technology resources available for teachers to access this online treasure? Would they have time in their busy schedules to even begin investigating and integrating these materials into their curriculum? Would I be able to guide them?

After actively promoting the American Memory resources for several years, my answer to all of these questions is a resounding "Yes!" The integration process takes time. Navigating though millions of documents is not an easy task. Learning "document analysis" requires practice. This term is a bit of a misnomer because in the world of primary sources, materials come in all formats—certainly documents, but also pictures and sounds. Understanding document analysis, however, is critical to the successful use of primary sources. So, too, is compiling either a virtual or printed "library" of primary resources for teachers to use, but none of this will not occur overnight. My advice is to begin slowly and proceed step-by-step. Even if teachers use only one primary resource at a time, this process will begin to affect student learning and understanding.

Document Analysis

So what is document analysis and why is it important? Document analysis is a structured way to view primary sources. It is what enables you as an educator to use primary sources in an instructive way. It requires students to actively engage in the learning process and form questions that guide further inquiry. The process can be summarized in three words: *observe, think,* and *ask.*

STEP 1: *Observe* carefully what can be seen in each photograph or item.

STEP 2: *Think* about what you are seeing. Connect it to what you or your students already know about the item. Use available clues. Often photograph descriptions or cataloging information add to what is observed.

STEP 3: *Ask* what additional information your students need to know to help them understand what they are seeing. How could they find answers to their questions?

The teachers and I usually model the process using several items that are not part of the classroom lesson. To keep things simple, we often provide students with graphic organizers to record their thoughts. A graphic organizer is a handout that helps children answer the three-part "observe-think-ask" document-analysis questions. There are several examples of graphic organizers on the Learning Page, which is discussed in some detail in chapter 8. We also discuss vocabulary words that will help the children understand the lesson.

Collaborate!

Collaboration between the librarian and the classroom teacher is another key to success. The American Memory Fellows Program realized the importance of this concept and solicited teacher-librarian partners as applicants. My fifth-grade colleague Doris Waud and I returned from our summer experience at the Library of Congress with a high level of enthusiasm and creative ideas. Each American Memory teacher-librarian team was asked to develop an online lesson that could be shared with other teachers.

Because 2000—the year of our fellowship—was also a presidential election year, Doris and I wondered how we could focus our elementary students' attention on women's voting rights. We wanted students to analyze American Memory documents and discover for themselves the strategies that women used to achieve the right to vote. Our lesson, "Voices for Votes: Suffrage Strategies," can now be viewed online on the Library of Congress Learning Page.[2]

WOMEN'S RIGHTS: MY MOM <u>NOT</u> VOTING?!

How could today's modern children begin to imagine their mothers' *not* having the right to vote? By examining the image, word, and auditory "pictures" found in the Library of Congress American Memory collections, our fifth-grade children came to understand that the right to vote had been a long, hard fight for women.

Assembling Primary Sources

We scoured the American Memory collections and printed out pictures and documents relating to the suffrage movement. We located early photos of women marching in parades, as seen in figure 5-2; giving speeches; and standing in picket lines. We found petitions, declarations, pamphlets, cartoons, postcards, advertisements, songs, and other items that documented strategies used in promoting the suffrage cause. We laminated our documents, making sure to include the bibliographic information on the back of each one.

As a pre-activity session, students brainstormed the kinds of strategies people used to influence others' opinions and thus effect change. We discussed this list and then reviewed unfamiliar election-related vocabulary. After a quick review of document analysis strategies (observe, think, and ask), we divided the class into small groups and distributed our primary-source documents.

Examining Primary Sources

In small groups, students were instructed to examine the documents and identify strategies used by suffragists to influence and change public attitudes about suffrage for women. Each group generated a list and shared it with the whole class. Lively discussion followed. In a culminating activity, the students selected a current voter-related issue, and, using one of the suffragists' strategies, designed a product, such as a poster, pamphlet, button or advertisement, to influence current public opinion. Figure 5-3 is a photograph of the children displaying their women's suffrage projects.

Extension activities included completing practice voter registration forms, writing persuasive letters to the local paper encouraging citizens to come out and

Figure 5-2
Suffrage parade in New York City, May 6, 1912. From *By Popular Demand: Votes for Woman Suffrage Pictures, 1850–1920,* American Memory collection.

vote, inviting a local candidate to speak, holding a mock election, compiling items for a class election scrapbook, and creating a class suffrage timeline museum.

The online version of our lesson provides links to all of the documents we used and includes detailed instructions for each activity. Not only did this activity incorporate the use of primary sources, but it also gave added meaning to the current election process.

CREATING PERSONAL SCRAPBOOKS

As we worked with primary sources, Doris and I both realized that students need an understanding of *their* past before they can make connections to our nations' collective history. We turned to the familiar American hobby of creating scrapbooks through which stories of the past are revealed.

Figure 5-3
Elementary school children enjoy examining primary-source documents from the American Memory collections and discussing the issues associated with women earning the right to vote.

Examining Old Scrapbooks in Class

Doris decided to have each child in her fifth-grade class compile a personal yearlong scrapbook. To give the children some ideas, I visited her class at the beginning of the school year and brought a variety of old scrapbooks with me. Like many teachers, I am an avid collector. In my antique shop travels, I had purchased several old scrapbooks for the students to examine. A worn leather-covered album featured nineteenth-century photographs. A Victorian "scrap" album contained colorful old advertisements. My family scrapbook and my daughter's 1970s sticker collection album engaged their interest. We encouraged students to examine these scrapbooks.

Telling My Story

While discussing the scrapbook project, I related my own personal story. As a child, my father took constant pictures. In his work as researcher at Eastman Kodak Company, he used his four daughters as handy models for his projects. At our house, family photographs filled boxes, hung on walls, decorated Christmas cards, and were even displayed in commercial advertisements. It didn't take long for us to grow tired of serving as a captive photo crew. We complained, argued, and became irritable. I remember thinking to myself, "I will *not* make *my* children undergo this painful process."

DOCUMENTING MY STORY

Smiling, I then assured the class that, as an adult, I had changed my mind. I am now thankful that my father took these photographs. His images provide tangible evidence of the home we lived in, our immediate family, extended family, pets, hobbies, holiday celebrations, special moments, and even silly moments. These are primary sources that document *my* personal history. I described to them the overflowing boxes of photographs and miscellaneous documents that my mother had been saving in her basement to put in albums . . . someday! I told them how I spent several months sorting through the contents of this treasure and compiling individual albums for each of my sisters. I finished my story by showing them a copy of a finished album.

Sharing my personal story helped the children make connections. Children find it difficult to imagine that teachers were once young like themselves. Her students laughed at the "funny-looking" clothes my parents wore in the 1940s. Photos of my relatives that came to America from Holland through Ellis Island brought meaning to the immigrant experience they were currently studying. Viewing a photograph of my grandfather's farm family near Boonville, New York, sparked questions about its location. Comparing my father's chronological series of holiday family photo cards gave them a sense of my growing-up years. Observing my personal album, as well as the other types of antique scrapbooks they had seen, proved to be an effective hook.

Children Tell Their Stories

The children were anxious to get started. Creating their own albums and encouraging them to save photos, movie tickets, menus, letters, news articles, and product labels from their own experiences helped them understand the relevance of primary sources that would provide future clues to their own past. Students added to their scrapbooks throughout the year. Their finished end-of-year projects were treasures for each of them.

At the end of the school year, we arranged a videoconference with curators in the Library of Congress Rare Books Division where the Susan B. Anthony scrapbooks are held. (You will learn more about the Library's videoconferencing program in Chapter 8.) The students learned about scrapbook conservation techniques and shared their personal scrapbooks with Library of Congress staff. The students were so enthused after this experience that we decided to have them examine examples of historical scrapbooks that are available on the American Memory website.

Examining Historical Scrapbooks

If you don't have your own albums to share with the children, or if you wish to integrate this activity with a specific historical era, consider using the American Memory collections. To locate scrapbooks, use the search words, "album" or "scrapbook." This search will result in hundreds of hits. For example, *The Frederick Douglass Papers* includes a scrapbook of newspaper items, photographs, letters, and other memorabilia related to the abolitionist. The *Samuel F. B. Morse Papers* contains an album of bound clippings related to the development of the telegraph. The *Words and Deeds in American History* collection has a Civil War album with photos of over two hundred Civil War officers and political and cultural figures of the period. The *Emergence of Advertising in America* collection features four nineteenth-century Victorian scrapbooks with hundreds of advertising trade cards, greeting cards, token of affection cards, calling cards, railroad tickets, social invitations, and other ephemera of the era.

Students can view these online albums in class, in the computer lab, or at home with their own computer. Exploring scrapbooks online is almost like holding the genuine thing, and can be combined with classroom activities like those described earlier. Typically, the first image is of the binder, often a gilded leather binder. Individual items are shown as they appear on the scrapbook page.

THE VALUE OF OFFLINE MATERIALS

Files can also be downloaded and saved to the hard drive or CD-ROM for later use. Printing out and laminating documents saves time for future lessons. When lab access is not available or technological difficulties occur, saved or printed copies will come in handy. I have been gradually building my personal "hands-on" collection of scrapbook items and other primary source documents. I have found them to be invaluable in both student and adult teaching situations. Although viewing a document online is far less time-consuming than creating documents for hands-on use, the tactile aspect of actually handling an item often makes for a more authentic experience.

OTHER ACTIVITIES AND TOPICS FOR ELEMENTARY SCHOOL

Halloween

Halloween is a day that is hard to ignore in elementary school. Even if special activities are not planned, students still get excited about the event. Doris came up with a primary source scavenger hunt and a creative writing exercise using Halloween themes.

We searched the American Memory collections using words such as "tomb," "gravestone," "headstone," and "casket." We selected twenty-five images, printed them, and mounted each picture on gray paper cut in the shape of a tombstone. We numbered the tombstones, placed bibliographic and descriptive information on the back of each image, and developed a set of questions that students could answer by careful observation of the photos. We also created a vocabulary list of new or unfamiliar words that the students might encounter during the activity.

Before we began the actual lesson, we reviewed the document-analysis steps discussed earlier in this chapter. And then the fun began! We placed the paper tombstones on a large table and started the students scavenging the images for clues. They were fascinated by the photos and completed the task in a surprisingly short time.

After sharing the correct answers and awarding sleuthing prizes, each student selected one photo to use as the basis for creative writing. We asked them to imagine themselves standing within the picture and, from that point of view, to write a paragraph about what they saw, how they might have felt, and what they wondered about. The resulting "Tombstone Tales" were posted in the hall and proved to be a popular display of student work for the rest of the school.

America's Symbols: September 11

When the tragic events of September 11, 2001, occurred, American flags, banners, ribbons, and other patriotic symbols appeared everywhere. This tragedy inspired us to develop an activity that explores symbols through the American Memory collections.

CELEBRATE AMERICA!

Doris wanted to help her students understand how visual symbols came to represent the spirit of America. We also wanted the children to consider what being an American meant to them. The American Memory collections are full of images of America's symbols. Photos of famous monuments like the Liberty Bell, Plymouth Rock, the Statue of Liberty, and the Presidential Seal are a few examples. Doris printed out a dozen documents and developed a worksheet for students to use as they analyzed the symbols. Pairs of students selected one document, and, with the help of reference books, completed the worksheets and wrote reports about their chosen symbol.

NEW SYMBOLS FOR AMERICA?

As an extension activity, students created original symbols in the form of a pledge, poem, or visual symbol that would have meaning in the twenty-first century. Students used historical primary-source documents for inspiration, and then thought about the present by creating their own symbols. Rory designed a visual of several wolves that was accompanied by the following explanation: "I chose the wolf as a new symbol for America because it represents the strength of the U.S.A. Like a wolf pack, the U.S. is strongest when people come together."

Immigration: Scrapbooks, Role Playing, and Postcards

What elementary school does not have a unit on immigration in the curriculum? As part of our fifth-grade curriculum, students search the American Memory collections for Ellis Island documents and photographs to illustrate pages of a class immigration scrapbook. Students then take on the role of immigrants and dress in costume. Family members, school staff, and other classes are then invited to interview them about their "immigrant" experiences. To make it seem "more real," a 1903 Library of Congress silent film from the Edison Company, *Emigrants Landing at Ellis Island,* is projected from the classroom computer during the event. (See figure 2-12.)

HISTORICAL FICTION AND CREATIVE WRITING

Another Fyle fifth-grade teacher, Lisa Cooke, also uses primary-source photographs to add depth to the immigration topic. As part of her unit, students read historical novels about the period.[3] Upon completion of the reading, students are given printed photos from the American Memory collections, and they select one of the photos to work with.[4] Acting as the main character in the book they read, they write a picture postcard to their "imaginary" relatives based on the selected photograph. In their message, they need to include descriptions of the immigrant's travels, experiences, homes, and jobs. The also have to describe what life was like for the main character. Careful observation of these primary-source photos provides a perfect springboard for creative writing and gives students a broader understanding of the difficulties that immigrants faced. Read this insightful student postcard based on the image in figure 5-4. Spencer writes as the fictional character of Otto to his parents in Finland:

Figure 5-4
Immigrants on an Atlantic liner. This 1906 image appears in the Library of Congress Prints and Photographs Online Catalog.

Dear Family, Tis very different in the New World. Twas very different what we as a family have thought it was. The streets are dirty. The clothes hang from the windows. The work here is hard labor. The journey across the sea alone was deadly. Many of the immigrants passed away on the voyage. We had such little space and food. I heard that a ship sunk in the storm we endured.

The Pioneer Experience: Through Biography and Photographs

Other teachers use similar techniques with different topics. For example, when Ann Looby's fourth-grade students at Fyle studied pioneer life, she read them *Prairie Visions: The Life and Times of Solomon Butcher* (Pam Conrad, Darryl S. Zudeck, and Solomon Butcher).[5] Solomon Butcher was a photographer who migrated to Nebraska in 1880, photographed prairie families, and collected their true stories. Many of his photographs appear in the American Memory collection, *Prairie Settlement: Nebraska Photos and Family Letters, 1862–1912* (see figure 5-5). After reading the book, Ann asked the students to create picture postcards from the images found in American Memory. Assuming the role of a pioneer trav-

Figure 5-5
Samuel Butcher photographing children at Broken Bow, Nebraska. This photograph appears in *Prairie Settlement: Nebraska Photos and Family Letters, 1862–1912*, American Memory collection.

eler, the students' messages told their family or friends back home about the people, buildings, or activities in the picture they chose. Final products were shared with the class and posted in the hall.

What Does Freedom Mean?

Ann Looby is currently teaching fourth grade at the Genesee Community Charter School at the Rochester Museum and Science Center in Rochester, New York. Her colleagues at this expedition-based school, Lisa Wing, school leader, and Lisa O'Malley, also realize the importance of integrating primary sources into the curriculum.

GUIDING QUESTIONS

Their "Freedom Expedition" project focused on two guiding questions: *What is freedom? What are the responsibilities that come with being free?* The Bill of Rights, Underground Railroad, women's rights, and civil rights were topics of historical study during the unit.

Teachers gathered primary-source documents, including photos of a slave ship, a sketch of Harriet Tubman being taken as a child from her family, a slave receipt, a photo of a Civil War drummer boy, an anti-suffrage button, and a fugitive-slave poster, for the students to examine.

The culminating project featured a presentation in which each student assumed the role of a character from the period. They dressed as that person might have dressed, and while a slide of a related primary source was projected on a large screen, each student reacted in character to the document.

For example, as the visual of a slave receipt shown in figure 5-6 is projected on the screen, a student acting in the role of Harriet Tubman recites:

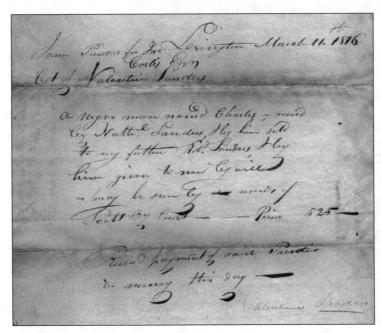

Figure 5-6
Sales receipt (1816) for an African-American slave named Charles, from the Corlis-Respess family papers. This image is found in *First American West: The Ohio River Valley, 1750–1820*, American Memory collection.

Can you believe it! That there is a receipt for a human being. No different than a sack of feed or a hog for the farm. It brings tears to my eyes to know all the suffering my people had to endure. I was born a slave, but they could not chain my spirit. I escaped!! Life has more value than a piece of paper. The efforts of the abolitionists made the sale of my people illegal in this country of ours. Thank our Lord!

A visual slide of an issue of Frederick Douglass's newspaper, *North Star*, is projected on the screen while another student, in the role of Frederick Douglass, narrates:

My newspaper was named for the star that helped us get to the North. When I wrote my paper, I gave it a lot of thought. I spent many hours fixing my mistakes and reading it over. It was a newspaper for black people, but I wanted to make it the best so white people against me couldn't say it was a dumb newspaper. I had many people help me with the paper. John Brown, a conductor in the railroad, was by my side. My paper is still published today in Rochester, New York.

THE ROLE OF THE LIBRARY MEDIA SPECIALIST

These classroom and library anecdotes demonstrate that American Memory can be a gold mine of primary-source materials for elementary school teachers. What can library media specialists do to spread the word and encourage the use of primary sources? While my current experience is in elementary school, the same principles apply to middle school and high school. Think about the multifaceted role of the librarian as described in *Information Power*—the librarian as information specialist, instructional partner, teacher of students, and program administrator.[6] Assume each of these roles and broadcast the American Memory word.

Information Specialist and Instructional Partner

Librarians have been trained to identify and gather appropriate resources that will help teachers deliver the curriculum and engage students in learning. The American Memory collections are vast, and teachers have little time to peruse them at their leisure. If you are a librarian, ask teachers what subjects are lacking in primary source material.

Browse the collections with your school curriculum in mind (a sampling is shown on page 85). Become familiar with the writing genres taught throughout the curricula. When journaling or diary writing is being taught, locate examples from the collections that might fit in with this writing genre. When Women's History Month is approaching, familiarize teachers with relevant collections in American Memory that would relate to the topic. Use every method possible to increase your teachers' and students' information literacy about primary sources, how to access and understand them.

E-mail is an invaluable tool for keeping teachers up-to-date with American Memory happenings. As you become aware of historical periods being studied,

> ## More Curriculum Connections for Elementary School
>
> **Native Americans:** *American Indians of the Pacific Northwest*
> http://memory.loc.gov/ammem/award98/wauhtml/aipnhome.html
>
> **American Revolution:** *The American Revolution and Its Era*
> http://memory.loc.gov/ammem/gmdhtml/armhtml/armhome.html
>
> **Civil War:** *Selected Civil War Photographs Collection*
> http://memory.loc.gov/ammem/cwphtml/cwphome.html
>
> **Pioneer Life:** *Northern Great Plains, 1880–1920*
> http://memory.loc.gov/ammem/award97/ndfahtml/ngphome.html
>
> **Women Suffrage:** *By Popular Demand: "Votes for Women" Suffrage Pictures, 1850–1920*
> http://memory.loc.gov/ammem/vfwhtml/vfwhome.html
>
> **The West:** *History of the American West, 1860–1920*
> http://memory.loc.gov/ammem/award97/codhtml/hawphome.html
>
> **World War I:** *American Leaders Speak: Recordings from World War I and the 1920 Election*
> http://memory.loc.gov/ammem/nfhtml/nfhome.html

make an effort to notify teachers of American Memory collections that would tie in with their units. E-mail messages take only a few minutes, and if even one teacher follows up your messages and uses the information, consider your efforts to have been a success.

PROACTIVE SCHOOL LEADER

Once you get started working with teachers, share your successes proactively. Think about setting up a building "study group" and get together after school to build a shared resource file of primary sources. Create a set of web links to frequently used American Memory activities and resources and make them available on your school or library website. Teach other teachers in your district about American Memory by offering in-service sessions to showcase these treasures. Most important, continue to explore! New collections and features are added to the Library of Congress site on a daily basis. If you, as the librarian, are the first to discover a newly added site, spread the word to your colleagues. Do what you do best: highlight important resources for teachers and students in your school to use.

CHEERLEADER FOR PRIMARY SOURCES

In addition to collaborating with teachers in your own school, become a cheerleader for primary sources. Contribute to regional and state workshops. Set up a "Get Tech Day" and develop a website to showcase American Memory collections, features, and activities. Students and teachers throughout the area can "visit" the Library of Congress links via this website and became part of the American Memory community of users. Volunteer to present at your public library or local college.

TEACHER OF STUDENTS

Navigating the American Memory collections can be a challenge for all age levels, but especially for elementary students. Collections can be confusing and search terms can be unfamiliar. Before you send students off on American Memory searches, try the search yourself. What collections will best meet students' needs? What search terms will be most successful in retrieving documents that will fit with the assignment at hand?

ONLINE COACH

Work with the classroom teacher to define exactly what types of documents would help the students the most. What search strategies can they understand? Give the students a chance to experiment, and be there to help them if they have questions. Working together—librarians, teachers, and students—will provide the best results.

ARBITRATOR FOR DIFFICULT MATERIALS

An important consideration as you spread the American Memory word is that all documents in the collections reflect the social settings of the times in which they were written. Language used mirrors the language and social values of the period. Cultural biases are often evident in primary sources. Vocabulary used might be offensive in today's world. In your role as librarian and teacher, it is important to remind students to be aware of this fact.

As you introduce collections and primary sources to students, encourage your students to be sensitive to the language used in the documents they explore. Ask them to consider how and why this language might no longer be acceptable.

Program Administrator

While using primary sources is only one part of a librarian's job, it is one that can raise the visibility of the library and its resources while also highlighting school-wide projects. In fact, teachers and students have come *to expect* school libraries to be the place where schoolwide projects are highlighted.

To showcase American Memory resources, try rotating displays of photos and documents outside of your library. Prior to the 2000 elections, I created a "Great Wall of Presidents" photo quilt featuring prints and photos of all of America's presidents from the Library of Congress collection *By Popular Demand: Portraits of the Presidents and First Ladies*. Photos were arranged in chronological order and names of presidents and their dates of office were listed under the portraits. In conjunction with the display, I initiated a schoolwide activity challenging students to use their observation skills to answer a dozen presidential "observation questions."

The American Memory collections have photos and documents that can be used for similar displays throughout the year. During American Education Week I searched the collection for photos of early schools or one-room schoolhouses and posted some of the wonderful photos that I found. I followed this display with Thanksgiving images and other documents to highlight the holiday season. The 2002 Presidential Inauguration was a perfect opportunity to showcase items from the collection *I Do Solemnly Swear . . . Presidential Inaugurations*. When David Schwartz, author of popular children's math-related picturebook titles, including *If You Made a Million, How Much Is a Million* and *G Is for Googol*, made a 2002 visit to Fyle School, I created an "I Spy Shapes and Numbers in American Memory" exhibit. Searching the collections for mathematical terms like "circle," "square," "graph," and "calculate" yields fascinating results. Just tapping into the American Memory Today in History feature (http://memory.loc.gov/ammem/today/today.html) can provide images and documents that connect to every day in the school year. The possibilities are endless. All it takes is imagination and a bit of time to expose your students to these riches. Use these as starter ideas and come up with new ones of your own.

Once you—and your colleagues—get started using the collections, the American Memory fan club will explode. You will have silenced the skeptics about using primary sources with elementary school children. If these classroom vignettes tell you anything, they tell you that the power of "story" is a great motivator for student learning.

NOTES

1. Search on "Waud" to find this image in *Selected Civil War Photographs, 1861–1865* [online], available at http://memory.loc.gov/ammem/cwphtml/cwphone.html.

2. "Voices for Votes: Suffrage Strategies" [online], available from http://memory.loc.gov/ammem/ndlpedu/lessons/00/suffrage/index.html.

3. Suggested reading includes Barry Denenberg, *So Far from Home: The Diary of Mary Driscoll, an Irish Mill Girl* (New York: Scholastic, 1997); Karen Hesse, *Letters from Rifka* (New York: Holt, 1992); William Durbin, *The Journal of Otto Peltonen: A Finnish Immigrant* (New York: Scholastic, 2000); and Kathryn Lasky, *Dreams in the Golden Country: The Diary of Zipporah Feldman, a Jewish Immigrant Girl* (New York: Scholastic, 1998).

4. An excellent set of selected Ellis Island images in the Library of Congress collections can be found at http://lcweb.loc.gov/rr/print/070_immi.html.

5. Pam Conrad, Darryl S. Zudeck, and Solomon Butcher, *Prairie Visions: The Life and Times of Solomon Butcher* (New York: HarperCollins, 1991).

6. American Association of School Librarians (AASL) and Association for Educational Communications and Technology (AECT), *Information Power: Building Partnerships for Learning* (Chicago: ALA, 1998).

CHAPTER SIX

History Told Firsthand in Middle School

LAURA WAKEFIELD

I have always loved to learn about America's history—as I heard it firsthand from my grandmother. I remember her telling me about what it was like to live on the east coast of Florida during World War II. People feared that German spies might come ashore from submarines (figure 6-1), so all bridges leading to the mainland were guarded. At night, friends and neighbors would gather on the beach to watch the gun battles between ships at sea. Her war stories told about everyday life and the sacrifices that the family made as well. For example, she took my Dad and his brother to stay with relatives in the Tennessee mountains each summer because in those days, before the polio vaccine, people believed a cooler climate prevented the dreaded disease. During the war, the rationing of gas and tires, however, meant in order to save enough gasoline to drive to Tennessee, the family had to walk everywhere else.

As a child, I was fascinated by these stories about my family's experiences during the war. Yet, at school, history was boring. We read the chapter, answered the questions at the end, and took a multiple-choice test. It seemed that there was so much information to cover that there was no time to slow down and discover the human drama hidden behind the dry recitation of facts.

As a teacher, I wanted something better for my eighth-grade American history students. I wondered how I could re-create for them the experience I had listening to my grandmother's stories. I wanted my middle school students to experience history as I did at home—firsthand. Simply having them read material would

---

Laura Wakefield is a teacher in Kissimmee, Florida.

Figure 6-1
World War II poster urging Americans to loan their binoculars to the Department of the Navy. From *By the People, For the People: Posters from the WPA, 1936–1943,* American Memory collection.

not work. Each year, the reading abilities of my nearly 180 middle school students range from second to eleventh grade. More students read below grade level than above grade level. Up to 20 percent are handicapped by attention deficit disorder or diagnosed with learning disabilities. For nearly 30 percent, English is a second language. How could I incite these students to become excited about learning history?

I decided to teach my students how to discover their *own* family histories by talking with their parents. My students would learn how to interview family or friends and then write that individual's "oral history" by using historical artifacts of all sorts from the Library of Congress American Memory collections. Using the American Memory collections, my students would *become* historians.

MEMORY, REASON, AND IMAGINATION

As a teacher, I was drawn to Thomas Jefferson for inspiration. Thomas Jefferson, whose library formed the original collection of the Library of Congress, organized his personal library into three types of knowledge: Memory (History); Reason (Philosophy); and Imagination (Fine Arts). Couldn't this structure also provide a model for a well-rounded history curriculum? If I can create an environment in which my students can explore the role of memory in their own lives, I am convinced that history will become more relevant to them. Without reason, however, memory has no context. To understand the past, we need to relate memory to reason—to help students make sense of past events within the context of their own times. The other ingredient crucial to this mix is imagination. Imagination provides a medium for reaching memories and sharing them. If my teaching reflects these ideals, my students will know that shared memories are the core of a common national past, and they will be able to use their imagination and reason to understand the human drama that makes up our nation's history. For what is history if not a great story told?

Just as Jefferson's library became the foundation of the Library of Congress, the American Memory collections provided the base for me to draw upon memories, develop historical reasoning, and tap my students' imaginations. This chapter describes how the fascinating primary-source documents, images, and ephemera found in the American Memory collections have fired up my middle school students about history.

INTRODUCING ORAL HISTORY

I began "The Living History Project" in 1997 in collaboration with my Library of Congress American Memory Fellow partner, Joy Penney, who at the time taught gifted students at the same school where I continue to teach, Neptune Middle School in Kissimmee, Florida. Joy and I were convinced that the American Memory collections could work with all kinds of students, my "regular" students, who ran the gamut from learning disabled to average, or Joy's gifted students.

This project begins with a deceptively simple activity: teaching students how to analyze photographs. Why *begin* an oral history project with visual materials? Photo analysis is a great method to connect memory, reason, and imagination in history. Photographs evoke memories, and memories are what oral history is all about. We want students to see that they can learn about the past from family members who have experienced it. Once students have learned the principles of photo analysis and interview skills, they can conduct oral histories.

We titled the first lesson in this project "Transplants: Stories of Individuals Who Migrated to Central Florida." Because most people in the area of central Florida where we live came from somewhere else, we felt this theme was broad enough so that students with varying skills and abilities could succeed. Through the process of collecting oral histories, we hoped students would strengthen their personal communication skills while learning about diverse experiences of people in the area. Also, we believed it was important to document the changing demographics of our region through the life stories of individuals who now call central Florida home. This lesson and other materials we developed as American Memory Fellows are available on the Library of Congress Learning Page.[1]

In looking back, I am amazed at what students accomplished. I required them to select a "transplant" to interview, conduct a tape-recorded interview of that person detailing his or her life history, transcribe the interview word-for-word, and turn it in along with a photograph of the individual. All my students completed the task (that alone is exceptional), and, with very few exceptions, the life histories were fascinating reading——providing compelling slices of American history. See, for example, this excerpt from a student's interview of her grandmother, who recollects her experiences during World War II in Sidney, Australia.

> Then I asked her about World War II. She said she was on the living room floor reading the comic strip "Maggie and Jiggs" when the announcement was made on the radio that Sunday. Soon after the war began, my grandmother went to work in a defence factory in Sidney called Bendix Aviation, and had many jobs. My grandmother was a micro-inspector, wound coils for airplanes, ran turret lathes, operated gear-cutting machines, making ring gears, pinion gears, and also worked on a magnaflux (a process to check to see if the gears had any cracks in them). I asked her about ration books and she said they had ration books for items like shoes, gas, butter, and cigarettes. The government gave you an A or B stamp for gas, but she had both because she drove people to work.

Students consistently reported that conducting these interviews was the hardest task they had ever accomplished and the one of which they were most proud. How did my students acquire the skills necessary to accomplish this task?

TEACHING PHOTO-ANALYSIS SKILLS

A Starting Point for Oral Histories

Photo analysis is a productive starting point for this project for several reasons. As noted earlier, photographs evoke memories, and with the wide range of photos online, you can find photographs on many topics. Thus, teacher preparation is easy. The photo-selection process is made even simpler by the gallery-view feature in American Memory, which allows the viewer to see a small version of each photo quickly. Time is not wasted opening multiple photos that do not contain the desired material. Photo analysis is nonthreatening. It appeals to students—even to students with learning disabilities and problems—since today's students are highly visually oriented.

Introducing Photo Analysis

Despite its advantages, photo analysis is not without difficulties. Students' interpretation of photographs depends heavily on their prior knowledge. That is why prior to examining a photo it is helpful to prepare students to think about what they might already know concerning the topic or era represented visually. Another factor influencing interpretation is the students' ability to decipher clues within a photograph. It is important to select photographs with multiple clues to appeal to the inevitable wide range of students' prior knowledge. Clues may include such factors as dress, technology, architecture, individual expression, surroundings, and transportation.

I like to begin immediately to set the stage. During the first week of school, I share with students some of my own elementary school experiences in the south prior to school integration. I then require the students to ask their parents about their school experiences—how it was different then from now. I suggest that they ask their parents questions about school rules, materials, or lunches if they need help to jog their memories.

This assignment helps students begin to use their own background knowledge about school while acquainting them immediately with interviewing techniques. Another benefit is that it allows parents and students to talk together about their family history. Usually, students are fascinated to learn about their parents' school experiences and how they differ from their own. Students begin to learn that the interview they are conducting is a primary source. The next day we have a class discussion in which the students share their parents' experiences.

Using American Memory Resources

In the meantime, I look in the *America from the Great Depression to WWII* American Memory collection for photos. I choose black-and-white photographs from the Farm Security Administration, and then conduct a search with the keyword "school." This search produces multiple photos of depression-era school scenes. I limit my search to black-and-white photographs because they can be duplicated easily if additional copies are needed. This saves on computer printer ink cartridges—something for which my school has only limited funds. I select a number of photographs and make two sets to use with the class.

I explain to the students that today they are going to be historians examining a primary-source image. We review previous discussions we have had about what constitutes a primary source, making sure to identify photographs as primary sources. I explain that historians must have the ability to "read" pictures that might provide valuable information not available in written or oral histories.

Modeling the process of photo analysis with the whole class is essential. First, I project a transparency of a photograph of a rural classroom (figure 6-2) to analyze with the group.[2] Sometimes, I will make enough copies of the photo so each student has one to examine. This part of the activity is enhanced if you provide students with magnifying glasses and white cotton gloves. I explain to the students that archivists at the Library of Congress put on gloves before handling many original documents and photographs to prevent smudges or oils from the skin from damaging the artifacts. You can demonstrate by putting on gloves yourself before handling the photos. This has the added advantage of protecting the printed photos from student mishandling as well. Often magnifying glasses can be borrowed from a science teacher, or you can purchase inexpensive, plastic ones from an educational supply store. Middle school students feel like real detectives if they can pore over a photo with a magnifying glass!

Figure 6-2
Rural school in Williams County, North Dakota, in which an epidemic of "scabies" broke out. From *America from the Great Depression to World War II: Black-and-White Photographs from the FSA-OWI, 1935–1945,* American Memory collection.

USING A PHOTO-ANALYSIS SHEET

I also give each student a modified photo-analysis worksheet that was originally developed for the Library of Congress American Memory Fellows Institute. You can find a copy of this worksheet and others like it on the Learning Page. The American Memory Fellows developed worksheets such as these, which are available online for teachers to use as is or modify to suit individual instructional needs. Students use this worksheet to record their observations about the photograph.[3]

The first column on the photo-analysis guide is "observation." Students report what they see in the photo in this column. I caution students that they cannot make assumptions in this step. They are only to list what they see. Students might list "two boys, two girls, one woman, student desks, old fashioned telephone, large round object," or the like. I am always amazed at how many different things students will see in the photograph and how vehemently they will defend their view of what is in the picture. For example, this picture usually produces heated discussion of whether there are two women, or one woman and a reflection.

The second column of the photo-analysis worksheet is titled "knowledge." In this step, students apply reasoning to the process. Students list what they know that might be related to the image. Recalling prior knowledge, students make assumptions based on experience. This is also where information from the caption may be incorporated into their knowledge. The caption for this photograph generates a discussion of the meaning of "scabies." I inform the students that scabies is an infectious skin disease caused by a mite, which burrows under the skin and causes intense itching. For middle school students, this caption makes the picture highly interesting, since anything they consider gross or disgusting is intriguing. Students then typically write statements like the following:

"The children are in school, the woman is their teacher."

"The large round object is a stove. It might be winter because the people are wearing long sleeves."

Finally, the third column is titled "interpretation." In this column, students deduce what is happening in the picture. There are often differences in students' conclusions. One student might write:

"The health nurse is telling the teacher who has scabies and the children are curious to know who might have to go home."

I especially like the last section at the bottom of the page labeled "Further Research," which prompts the students to consider what further questions the photo has raised. Typically, students have many unanswered questions about the photo to discuss. I tell students that primary sources often raise more questions than they answer. Some students find it frustrating to learn that there is no unequivocal correct answer to this activity. Many ask me who in the classroom is "right." This allows me to discuss the notion of disagreement among historians and illustrates that historical research is often an ongoing process. In our discussion, I encourage students to think about the photographer who made the image and to ask themselves when and why the photo was taken. Through this exercise, they learn that primary sources are not necessarily objective. They realize that instead, photographs are often subjective, taken to convey a particular message.

CONSTRUCTING MEANING

Next, I divide students into small groups of no more than four students. Each group examines a photograph of a school scene—there are two sets of the same photographs, so more than one group will examine each photo—and the students work cooperatively to complete the analysis of their photograph. In their groups, I encourage students to express their thoughts about the photograph aloud to help construct meaning. Having students support their ideas with contextual knowledge or with clues within the photograph discourages wild guesses and inferences. This is followed by an opportunity for each group to share its analysis with the class. Because I have randomly distributed the two sets of photographs, each group has a chance to see how another group interpreted the same photo. Through this activity, students learn that one primary source can yield different perspectives. Photo analysis allows students to be very engaged. It has the added advantage that it is an assignment in which even students with limited English can participate.

A PICTURE IS WORTH 150 WORDS!

The culmination of the photo-analysis exercise is a homework assignment in which students write their own 150-word descriptions of what is happening in a given photograph. The purpose of this is twofold. First, it allows me to get a good early sample of student writing and to see how they construct their own interpretations of the photographs. Second, students enjoy using their imaginations to make sense of what they see in the photo and to share their creative ideas. Notice the depth of description in Allison's interpretation of the picture:

> All of the children wait for class to start. The teacher, Mrs. Honey, is being delayed by the principal, Ms. Jones, as she tells her how many students are out today by counting the empty seats. As they wait, Erica turns around in her chair to tell Cynthia about their new vice principal.
>
> The phone starts to ring, but Mrs. Honey is ignoring it. Steven blocks his mouth from view with his hand as he dares Jordan to run up and answer the phone. All of the children are dressed warmly in long sleeves, overalls, or long skirts so they don't catch a chill because the room is quite cold. Cynthia and Erica were patiently counting the minutes until they could get the games out of the second drawer of the chest.
>
> The empty seat belongs to Jessica, who left her scarf draped on her chair yesterday and forgot it. The black board has not yet been written on for the day's assignments so it remains blank at this time.

Clearly, images can add an important dimension to narrative and anecdotal accounts of the past. With visual skills honed, students are now ready to move on to the oral history portion of the project.

CONDUCTING ORAL HISTORIES

The photo-analysis activities introduce my students to the American Memory collections, to historical methodology, and to primary sources. The skills acquired through these activities will help students learn firsthand from their parents about the past. These experiences help set the stage for the oral history portion of "The Living History Project."

Oral history is a method of gathering historical information by interviewing an individual about his or her memories of past events. Collecting personal perceptions and recollections of history from a person with firsthand knowledge brings a vibrancy and immediacy to history. As a method of historical inquiry, the spoken memories of a person's life predate the written word. At the same time, documenting oral histories can be considered a modern technique, having received new life with the accessibility of tape recorders. Most of all, oral history is a compelling way to connect students with the past in a way that textbooks cannot. It makes history seem "more real" to middle school students.

Introducing Oral History

I have used a variety of techniques to spark student interest in oral history. Inviting local groups to visit the school and talk with the students is one excellent way to introduce oral history. I once invited a panel of local World War II veterans of the Japanese attack on Pearl Harbor to share their experiences of that fateful day with each of my classes. Students were fascinated by the veterans and enjoyed the opportunity to ask them questions.

I have also used recorded sound to introduce students to oral history. One recording I like to use is of an eye-witness account of Lincoln's Gettysburg Address which can be found on the National Public Radio website.[4] Now that students have experienced the traumatic national event of September 11, recordings from people in New York City on that fateful day may provide worthwhile teachable moments.

Another simple method is inviting a storyteller to weave magic in your classroom. I invited a colleague to visit the classroom and tell stories from her childhood. Because she was unable to visit all my classes personally, I videotaped her visit to my first period class and showed it the rest of the day. This worked well because the students quickly realized the potential for videotaping their own interviews. Whatever method you use, the goal is to enhance the students' interest in history and help them to see that they can conduct an oral history interview.

UNDERSTANDING THE 1930S

Once students have seen the power of history told firsthand, I introduce them to the experiences of Depression-era Americans through the work of the Federal Writers Project, an important New Deal program. The Library of Congress digital collection *American Life Histories Manuscripts from the Federal Writers Project, 1936–1940* includes many powerful first-person accounts of this era that students find fascinating. Interviews in this collection provide students with an oral history model and help them connect work done in the past to the assignment of writing their own life histories. Connections such as these are important because many of my students feel overwhelmed at the prospect of interviewing and transcribing a life history.

INTRODUCING THE COLLECTION

Many of the American Memory collections are difficult for middle school students to explore independently, and the *American Life Histories* collection is no exception. Most American Memory collections have "special presentations" that summarize or highlight the collection. Special presentations are usually accessible from the collection's home page. I began sharing selections from "Voices from the Thirties: An Introduction to the WPA Life Histories Collection."[5] This allows students to see the range of stories told—of hardship, adventure, and war, as well as stories of everyday life and work.

Another good starting point is the Collection Connections feature on the Learning Page. This feature is accessible from the Learning Page and also from each individual collection. It is an excellent resource that suggests a myriad of uses for the collection in the classroom.

And, finally, since most middle school students have never heard of the Federal Writers Project or the Work Projects Administration (WPA)—the federal program under which this project was sponsored—it is a good idea to provide a literary context. I begin by explaining that many of the writers (including Ralph Ellison, Richard Wright, Saul Bellow, and John Cheever) drew on their WPA interviews later when writing books that established their reputations. Because she lived nearby and set many stories in central Florida, I especially note that the African-American novelist and anthropologist Zora Neale Hurston was a WPA writer (see figure 6-3).

Figure 6-3
An Alan Lomax photograph of Floridian author Zora Neale Hurston, who wrote in the 1930s. From *African American Odyssey,* American Memory collection.

CHOOSING A LIFE HISTORY FROM THE COLLECTION

The next step is to take students online to search the *American Life Histories* collection for oral histories collected during the 1930s. Turning students loose in the collection can be a search-and-rescue operation! The students' first assignment is to select a life history that they find particularly interesting, analyze it, and then illustrate it with a suitable historical photograph. Through these activities I hope to develop students' ability to search online sources and to enhance their visual literacy skills. I take each class of students to the school technology lab to use the Internet. Depending on the computers available, students can be paired or work individually.

The first day, students are given a search worksheet to complete.[6] This form is designed to briefly familiarize novices with how to maneuver broadly within American Memory and, more specifically, with the *American Life Histories* collection. Like the photo-analysis form, this worksheet is also available online on the Learning Page.

On the second and successive days, students find a life history that interests them and analyze it. To assist in this task, they complete another worksheet. After noting that some life histories were too lengthy for students to read in the allotted time and that some students had difficulty finding one they liked, I began to preselect a limited number of life histories (three or four is usually enough for most classes) for them to choose from. (See the chart below for suggested life histories of interest to middle school students.) This activity typically takes students two 45-minute periods.

SUMMARIZING THE LIFE HISTORY

After analyzing the selected life history, each student must condense it into a short story and illustrate it appropriately, using photographs from the American Memory collections. There are several reasons I require the life history to be condensed. One is a practical reason: It is not possible for all of my 180 students to

Interesting Interviews for Middle School Students

I have found these interviews taken from the *American Life Histories Manuscripts from the Federal Writers Project, 1936–1940* are of particular interest to middle school students. The easiest way to find them is to type key words into the search box and select the search option, "Match exact phrase."

Interviews	*Search key words*
Berry-Picking An Adventure story about picking berries in South Carolina	*Berry picking*
The Blessed Candle The Civil War as experienced in Galveston, Texas	*Blessed Candle*
Mrs. John Donnelly Woman tells of the Northern Lights seen from a sod house on the Nebraska prairie	*Mrs. John Donnelly*
Rose Wilder Lane Daughter of Laura Ingalls Wilder tells of going west in a covered wagon	*Rose Wilder Lane*
Mrs. Annie E. Lesnett Woman tells about a mountain lion attack on a New Mexico farm	*Annie E. Lesnett*

print an entire life history selected from the American Memory collections at school because most are four or more pages in length. Requiring each student to condense the life history to one page not only simplifies printing, but it also allows me to see that each student has read and understood the life history. If a student has not read the life history, he or she will not know what part to exclude from the synthesized version, and, consequently, the story will not make sense. Condensing the life history, therefore, provides an important check for student understanding. And, illustrating the life history helps students connect the life history with the photo-analysis practice they have already done. Choosing a photograph that reflects the content of the life history also provides another way to ensure their understanding of the content. Finally, it foreshadows their own assignment to photograph the person they will ultimately interview. I find that life histories are engaging examples of literature, and the process of analyzing them stretches most of my students' (often limited) literacy skills.

Refining the Project

By the second year of the "Living History Project," I knew I needed the support and help of a language arts teacher. Fortunately, Kaye Whaley, the language arts teacher on my academic team, was willing to participate. She strengthened the literacy dimension so badly needed by our students and was invaluable in helping students with interviewing skills, writing, and reading comprehension. Perhaps most important, her participation helped students see that history is a language of literacy and allowed them to make connections between language arts and history. In addition, she provided fresh ideas and another perspective as together we devised ways to make things work.

HEROIC STORIES

We decided on a multifaceted theme for the second year: "Heroic Stories." Because heroes have a profound influence on individuals and cultures, we believed the theme could be instrumental in helping middle schoolers understand their role in society and their potential for making a positive impact. We also wanted to address the fact that many students are unable to differentiate between the concepts of "hero" and "celebrity." In one *World Almanac* survey, students from eighth through twelfth grade were asked to choose their heroes. The heroes named were predominantly actors, comedians, singers and songwriters, and sports figures. We realized that if students do not see themselves as potential achievers in one of these areas, then it is difficult for them to recognize and value the hero within themselves or within others in their school, family, or community. We hoped that the heroes theme for the "Living History Project" would show students that heroes come in all shapes and sizes, and that they need not be famous or wealthy. The project was designed for students to recognize and value the heroic traits of individuals around them. Students connected with members of their community while developing a greater respect for an older generation.

THE PERFORMANCE ELEMENT

We also decided to add a performance element to the project as a way to show-case students' work to the community. In addition to becoming historians by collecting oral histories, students would become authors and museum curators. With funds from our local educational foundation, we compiled students' heroic stories in an anthology and published a copy for each student. Each student also created a memorial exhibit to honor his or her chosen hero. The results were inspiring! In some cases, students chose someone in their own family to interview; in others, the hero was someone they had not known well prior to the interview. Interestingly, a number of students chose veterans as their heroes, and the published anthology of heroic stories includes some incredible accounts of wartime experiences. Here is an example of student work:

> On June 5, 1944, we started out across the English Channel, but it was so rough that they had to turn around. Everyone was sick. On June 6, 1944, before daylight we went back across the English Channel. There was stormy weather that morning, waves higher than a house. We didn't know if we'd make it to the shore. I was on a troop ship and then I was on a landing craft with about thirty soldiers.
>
> I jumped off the craft. The Germans had dug a trench, and we stepped into the deep trench. I was weighed down—the pack weighed about fifty-six pounds plus my ammunition and my rifle. We were being shot at as we jumped off the craft. Soldiers were trying not to drown and were being shot at by Germans in bunkers on the beach at the same time.[7]

Other stories included dramatic rescues, individuals overcoming obstacles, as well as stories of perseverance in spite of financial or health problems.

We rented the local arts center for a night and exhibited the memorials students had designed to honor their chosen heroes. Students created a wide variety of memorials, including timelines, collages, posters, paintings, slide presentations, and exhibits. The heroes, their families, and the community were all invited to the event, which we called the Living History Gala.

A JOURNEY OF SELF-DISCOVERY

What have my students learned from the "Living History Project"? Students didn't discover only the person they interviewed; they went on a journey of self-discovery about what they could accomplish. Here are their own words about what they learned:

> "I leaned many things, like that even the most seemingly ordinary person can be the greatest hero inside and in their past."—*Sarah*

> "I learned that if you pay attention to people and their stories you can learn a lot of interesting things."—*Nathan*

"I learned that old people have lives too. Also that things weren't that different when they were young."—*Jennifer*

"I learned that it is important to remember things from the past and that there are a lot of heroes in this world that we don't know about."—*Katie*

"I think that the hardest part was typing the transcript of the interview. The person I interviewed sure did talk a lot. My interview was an hour and a half. When I typed it, it was seven pages long."—*Christin*

"The hardest part of this assignment was trying to be calm during the interview. I am so shy that the interview was almost the hardest thing I ever did."—*Tiffany*

"What I learned is how some people struggled, lost their lives, everything they had for just one thing—freedom."
—*Seth*

As for me, I learned that students are capable of far more than I would have supposed and that academic excellence can be achieved through oral history.

NOTES

1. "Living History Project" can be found at http://memory.loc.gov/ammem/ndlpedu/lessons/97/florida/home.html.

2. Search on "scabies" in *America from the Great Depression to World War II: Black-and-White Photographs from the FSA-OWI, 1935–1945,* available at http://memory.loc.gov/ammem/fsahtml/fahome.html.

3. This photo-analysis sheet can be found at http://memory.loc.gov/ammem/ndlpedu/ lessons/97/photo/analysis.html.

4. "Lost and Found Sound," found at http://npr.org. The title is "Eyewitness at Gettysburg."

5. The presentation "Voices from the Thirties" can be found at http://memory.loc.gov/ammem/wpaintro/exhome.html.

6. "Examine a Life History Worksheet" is available at http://memory.loc.gov/ammem/ndlpedu/lessons/97/florida/examine.html.

7. Excerpted from "An American Hero: James W. Hair," student interview.

CHAPTER SEVEN

Focus on the Questions in High School

MICHAEL FEDERSPIEL

This was the day I had been anticipating for months. This was the day when I first tested a lesson plan using electronic primary sources with my high school students. It did not end the way I had hoped.

The previous summer I had spent a week in Washington, D.C., working with Library of Congress staff members to create a lesson for high school students on the conservation movement that used the Library of Congress's vast online holdings. I had this opportunity because I had been selected to be a Library of Congress American Memory Fellow to learn about the library's digital collections and to create a model lesson plan using those resources. The lesson that my team partner and I ultimately created is now available on the Learning Page.[1] But, getting to that point was a long and memorable journey.

The day I am remembering now was the day I first tried that lesson with my Midland High School American history students. The previous day, I told them we would meet at the computer lab. I was there early, with handouts prepared, ready to celebrate what I knew would be a successful day. Well, instead, I finished the hour angry and sadly disappointed. From the beginning the whole thing was a disaster. Kids had trouble logging on. Everyone seemed to have a question about something different at the same time, and what I assumed would be an hour-long activity clearly would take a week. And, of course, my colleagues had already booked our computer lab solid for the next month.

Now, many lessons and successes later, I realize it wasn't the students who failed that first day, or even the lesson plan; it was my lack of understanding what

---

Michael Federspiel is a social studies coordinator in Midland, Michigan.

it takes to create and facilitate a meaningful Internet primary-document lesson. My goal in this chapter is to share some suggestions about using primary electronic documents to enhance learning in a secondary classroom.

MY INTERNET RESOURCES JOURNEY

Over the years, in my university methods classes, like most middle school and high school history teachers, I was told that it was important to use primary documents with students. Doing so would help them understand the historical method, improve their critical-thinking skills, and motivate them to enjoy history. After all, hadn't many of us decided to become history teachers because we had been moved by historical places, artifacts, and ideas? Sadly, the discussion about *how* to use them was far too brief and took place before the Internet was commonplace in secondary education.

When I was hired, I received a thick notebook of publisher's resources that accompanied our textbook and a "good luck" wish from my supervisor. The notebook contained a few primary documents, such as texts of speeches or documents and some transparencies of photographs or works of art. I had already collected some facsimile documents (including the Declaration of Independence and the Gettysburg Address) printed on some pseudo-parchment paper and some posters of famous Americans. I knew it would be good to use these but was not sure how.

As time went on, I collected more and more primary sources—some actual artifacts and some commercially published resources. For the most part, I used these as diversions: I shared my collection of Civil War stereographic views when we discussed the Civil War; I showed slides of Dorothea Lange's and Walker Evans' Depression-era photographs that I made from old college textbooks; and I brought in some World War I posters purchased at a local flea market. The students showed interest in these, but I realized that there wasn't a whole lot of learning going on.

I began to question why it was I thought primary resources should be a part of my classroom. I knew that critical thinking could be enhanced using primary sources and that students could gain an understanding of and appreciation for the work of historians and the nuances of our past. But, I wasn't sure any of that was happening the way I was using my limited supply of resources. I decided to do something about it.

More Questions than Answers

Since my school year and curriculum began with the Civil War, I decided to start there. I had a handful of Matthew Brady stereoscopic views and some enlarged poster-size photographs showing soldiers, battlefields, and weapons. How would a historian use resources like this? There were not enough examples to say anything definitive. My small collection could only raise more questions than it could answer. Then I realized that was really what I should focus on—the questions. I put together a photograph-analysis sheet and had the kids complete it using a photograph from their textbook. It essentially asked them to identify what they saw (specific things),

state what they already knew about the photo's topic,

make conclusions based on what they saw and already knew,

identify key questions they would need answered before they could make additional conclusions.

I assumed this would be easy for the students to do. Was I ever wrong! They returned the next day a little confused, with more questions (about the worksheet, not the photograph) than answers. This taught me an important lesson: whenever you introduce a new skill-based activity, make sure you model it with the class before expecting the students to master it on their own. Using an overhead transparency of the analysis form and a slide projector, we worked together to master the skills needed. I blended what we learned in class about the Civil War with what they learned analyzing photographs and felt pretty good about my use of documents in this unit. I only wished that I had more photographs for them to consider.

Finding More Materials—Online!

It was about this time that a friend of mine asked me if I had ever visited the Library of Congress's American Memory collections on the World Wide Web. Online, he said, were hundreds of Civil War photographs. At this point in my career, the only technologies I was comfortable with were overhead projectors, VCRs, and slide projectors. But, the thought of accessing this trove of images intrigued me enough to learn how to log on and "visit" American Memory.

I was overwhelmed with what I found. There, at one site, were 1,118 Civil War photographs taken under the supervision of Matthew Brady. They showed scenes of military personnel, preparations for battle and battle after-effects, portraits of both Confederate and Union officers, and a selection of enlisted men. For years I had been working with about a dozen views; now I had access to over a thousand. How could I modify my assignment to make use of these resources?

Forming Hypotheses: What Do <u>You</u> Think?

I decided to extend what I had already been doing. Historians essentially do two things—they analyze evidence and they draw conclusions. My photo-analysis assignment taught students how to do the first. Now I needed something to teach them how to do the second. What I devised is not very sophisticated. I designed an activity that asked students to

select a Civil War topic they'd like to learn more about (e.g., a specific battle or weapon),

find images related to the topic,

make a hypothesis (supported by the photographic evidence) about the topic.

The activity simply asks students to form a hypothesis about a Civil War topic of their own choosing and to support it using photographs from the Brady digital collection. I knew they would need help with the technology because they needed to navigate around the site and conduct searches. They would have at their fingertips a potential abundance of resources, but if they couldn't conduct fruitful searches, they could not be successful in this activity. The first couple of times I tried this with classes I learned more than they did. They had more questions than I had answers, but with every question I learned something to help me improve the lesson the next time. Gradually it (and I) got better, and the kids became successful at learning about the war, how historians "create" written history, and how to use the American Memory collections.

Over time, my experiences with the Civil War photographs and the American Memory collections transformed the way I taught and used primary documents. With the Internet's vast resources came new challenges for me and probably for other history teachers, as described here.

WHY USE ELECTRONIC PRIMARY SOURCES?

Given that using electronic primary sources poses challenges to many veteran teachers, why should secondary history teachers struggle with these issues? There are several reasons. They do not vary much from the reasons "regular" primary resources can and should be used.

Electronic resources can make history come alive. Many history devotees' first experiences with the past were highly personal. They visited a place, heard family members tell stories, and held historical artifacts. Something took history out of the textbook and made it something they could understand on a personal level. Having students read, see, and manipulate the building blocks of history can provide just such an experience. Online, teachers and students alike have access to resources on virtually any topic increasing the likelihood of finding something to "touch" everyone.

Using primary resources develops critical-thinking skills. It's important to realize that the documents themselves do not necessarily foster creative thinking; rather, it's what the teacher has the students do with them. The ability to find more documents online and to consider and evaluate them fosters critical thinking.

Primary resources promote a deeper understanding of content. Too often the general survey information in textbooks leads to history being "a mile wide and an inch deep." Students seldom grasp the depth and complexity of an issue or topic. Delving into the particulars allows multiple perspectives to be identified and considered.

Electronic resources such as these are typically free and the number of items increases every day. Rarely do teachers have bulging budgets to purchase classroom resources; however, it is often possible to download useful items at no cost. At the American Memory site, there are millions of free pictures, maps, letters, and songs.

Students need to learn skills associated with evaluating and searching electronic sites. Years ago we taught students to use the *Readers' Guide to Periodical Literature* and how to use a card catalog. Those skills were as appropriate for those times as teaching Internet skills is now. Many kids will be familiar with the Internet, but few have been taught search skills and how to determine a site's reliability.

Using electronic primary resources often supports curriculum standards. Virtually all states either have adopted or are considering adopting standards for social studies curricula. In most cases, the use of primary documents—especially to promote critical thinking—is recommended, if not required. These same states typically have technology standards that mandate skills easily taught using electronic resources.

HOW CAN TEACHERS USE PRIMARY RESOURCES?

Teachers' circumstances, especially as they relate to technology, are varied, to say the least. Some teachers may be skeptical of computers; others (who have grown up using them) are very comfortable. Some teachers are blessed with student's having easy access to computer labs—or have computers readily available in their classrooms. Others might have to share computers with other staff members and find it impossible to have their students use computers under their supervision.

Regardless of your personal situation, there are ways you can (and should) consider using electronic resources. If you do not take advantage of this technology, you are severely limiting your resources unnecessarily and depriving the students of exposure to the footnotes and cornerstones of history.

There are many ways to do this. A few of the most common methods follow. Consider combinations of these to most effectively reach a range of students and abilities.

Single-Document Use

This is in many ways the easiest to do and takes the least amount of time. Using a single document is efficient and allows for great flexibility. The teacher can download and photocopy a manuscript, photograph, or map, and give all students a copy with an accompanying assignment. If doing this, it is essential that the "document" be powerful. A copy of Jefferson's rough draft of the Declaration of Independence (see figure 1-1 on page 5) or Lincoln's Gettysburg Address might work this way.[2] By using a color printer it is possible to make a document such as this look "real," which adds to its effectiveness.

To fully take advantage of a single document, it is important that teachers have the students do something with it. Appreciating it is fine, but to maximize its use, design an assignment that asks them to think—to analyze it, compare it to something else, write about it, use it to support an argument or hypothesis.

For example, consider the photograph of this wooden shack (see figure 7-1) and what you could have kids do with it.[3]

Could students

> compare this family's home to the one described in Laura Ingalls Wilder's stories?
>
> describe what life would be like (in all seasons) for a family living here?
>
> speculate on how life here might be different from the life these people had before moving to the Great Plains?

Figure 7-1
Home is where the heart is. What thoughts do details in this image evoke? This image
can be found in *Northern Great Plains 1880–1920,* American Memory collection.

create a fictional diary written by the young boy?

explain what the items they see are used for?

Multiple Documents or Document Sets

When access to technology is limited and a teacher wants to expose students to
multiple artifacts on a single topic, document sets make sense. To give students a
sense of the reality of life on the Great Plains, I distribute sets of selected, printed,
and photocopied photographs that show scenes of town life, farming, housing, and
recreation.[4] Two photographs I like to use are those depicting an early twentieth-
century rural funeral and an 1894 prairie wedding (figures 7-2 and 7-3). These
scenes often will be in stark contrast to what many students associate with living
in the West. What sort of questions about home life and family gatherings might
be raised from these two images contrasted here? Imagine comparing these two
homes to ten other homes ranging from elaborate two-story wood frame struc-
tures to sod houses. What could the students learn about this time period with
such rich and varied views?

There can also be some nice connections established between single document
use and sets. Why not teach kids to "read" a photograph using a single Great
Plains image. Then, when they get a set of Great Plains images, they are prepared
not only to analyze the individual images but to also make some larger compar-
isons.

Document sets need not be exclusively photographs, or even documents with
similar original formats. Indeed, when creating document sets, teachers should
consider using a variety of genres. For example, if the class is studying the Civil

Figure 7-2
This simple rural funeral probably took place in North Dakota in the early 1900s.
What questions does it evoke? From *Northern Great Plains 1880–1920*, American
Memory collection.

Figure 7-3
This 1894 image depicts a prairie wedding in Milton, North Dakota. From *Northern Great
Plains 1880–1920*, American Memory collection.

Civil War Resources in American Memory

Band Music from the Civil War Era

Civil War Maps, 1861–1865

Horatio Nelson Taft's Civil War Diary, 1861–1865

The Frederick Douglass Papers at the Library of Congress, 1841–1964

Selected Civil War Photographs, 1861–1865

Abraham Lincoln Papers at the Library of Congress, 1850–1865

Abraham Lincoln and Civil War Sheet Music, 1859–1909

Walt Whitman Notebooks, 1850s and 1860s

Railroad Maps, 1828–1900

Presidential Inaugurations, 1789–2001

Broadsides and Printed Ephemera, 1600–2000

War, multiple collections and document formats could be accessed. See the sidebar for suggestions of additional American Memory Civil War resources.

Inquiry-Based Activities

Inquiry-based activities that provide students with independent research projects depend on student access to computers. They usually have more component parts, and, as a result, typically take longer to complete. If there is limited computer access, activities such as the one described next are impractical, if not impossible. If this is the case, you should focus on the single-document projects or creating document sets. For illustrative purposes, I'll refer to a lesson I developed on the Great Depression for classroom presentation that I later adapted for an American Memory professional development workshop.[5]

LEARNING ABOUT THE GREAT DEPRESSION

The Great Depression activity was used in conjunction with reading John Steinbeck's *The Grapes of Wrath* and took approximately a week to complete. It involved some classroom setup, two 50-minute class periods in the whole class computer lab, and a final product, which was turned in at the end of the week. My objectives were to have students

> learn about the styles and subjects of New Deal-era photographers,
>
> gain an appreciation of the reality of the Dust Bowl and migrant life,
>
> view some of the scenes that Steinbeck would have seen while researching *The Grapes of Wrath*, and
>
> learn about the purposes and accomplishments of the Farm Security Administration (FSA) and Office of War Information (OWI).

To complete the assignment, students needed to use the photographs found in American Memory in the collection *America from the Great Depression to World War II: Black-and-White Photographs from the FSA-OWI, 1935–1945.* I asked students to do two things—complete a worksheet about a Depression-era photographer and find images on an assigned topic relating to Steinbeck's text.

Before I took the students to the computer lab to begin their research, I spent time in the classroom getting them ready. Since we had already used the American Memory collections for previous assignments, I did not take time to explain how the site was organized or discuss search strategies. (Had we not already been familiar with it, I would have discussed these and modeled searches before they began.) They received a handout with step-by-step instructions and references to the necessary URLs. I suggested they visit the site on their own if they had Internet access at home in preparation for the next day in class.

When we arrived at the computer lab the next day, I began by using a projection unit to show the students the components of this particular site and to identify the key parts they would be using. Then they logged on and began to find images that illustrated the topic they had chosen (e.g., transportation, houses, roads, farms). I walked around the room, answering questions and making sure students were on task. They were expected to begin saving images they might want to use and to complete the first part of the lesson by the end of the hour. If they didn't, they could work on it at home or use the computers I have reserved after school.

The second day began again with instructions before students were allowed to turn on the computers. Lingering questions were answered, and the second day's task was explained again. Students worked to complete the assignment by the end of the period. Before the hour was over, I asked the students to shut down their computers, and I explained what they should do if they had not completed their tasks. The due date was the end of the week, so those who were not done would have a couple more days to complete the assignment.

The following week, we shared the results of the students' independent searches to find images that depict migrant life during the Dust Bowl to better understand the era in which John Steinbeck wrote the *Grapes of Wrath*. The students, having selected several images on their own time, such as abandoned farmhouses, as in figure 7-4, or refugees, as in figure 7-5, presented their choices to their classmates along with information about the photographer and why they had selected these particular images.

Figure 7-4
Dust storms ravage Oklahoma leaving abandoned farms such as this one. This image is found in *America from the Great Depression to World War II: Black-and-White Photographs from the FSA-OWI, 1935–1945,* American Memory collection.

Figure 7-5
In the same collection, you will find this image of Oklahoma drought refugees on a New Mexico highway.

WHAT DID I LEARN?

Okay, so what are the "lessons of this lesson" that can be transferred to other inquiry-based lessons? There are several, but four stand out:

Preparing students ahead of time is a key component for a successful lesson. The failed lesson description that began this chapter was a disaster primarily because I failed to prepare my students for the task ahead. Typically there is a great deal you can and should do ahead of time that will enhance the likelihood of a successful lesson. At a minimum, it is advisable to have a detailed handout prepared that identifies the lesson's objectives and gives key information (including step-by-step instructions and links that are needed). The instructor needs to decide whether or not this inquiry will involve only a selected site. There are often advantages to using only one site as it focuses all questions and answers on this single place. It can be very difficult to effectively respond to student questions if they are all unique to the various sites they are on (and they're all on different sites). It's also much easier to anticipate questions and avoid frustrations if all students are working on one site.

Modeling and helping students maintain focus while working at computers help them maximize what they accomplish on a day in the computer lab. Once students begin working on a computer, especially if it's with the rest of their classmates, it is easy for them to stray off topic and difficult for the teacher to focus all of them. Showing them the site *before* they begin work and anticipating where they will have problems and questions are a wise move. A little time spent doing this at the beginning of the hour saves a lot of eventual time.

Flexibility is important when dealing with Internet assignments. Experience has taught me that this is especially true when dealing with due dates. For a variety of reasons, I have found it difficult for all students to complete computer-related tasks within the amount of in-class time I allocate. By setting due dates later, I usually avoid problems with this while ensuring that students have the computer access necessary to complete the task.

Choice and accountability are important factors when designing inquiry activities. My students chose which of several photographers they wanted to learn more about and which images would illustrate their topic. I gave them ownership within my own parameters. Students generally tend to show more interest in assignments that allow them some ownership over the results. This is particularly true when doing Internet inquiries. I used the worksheet and posters to allow me to assess whether or not the students had achieved my desired objectives.

WHAT DID THE STUDENTS LEARN?

Primary documents are the building blocks of history and are open to—indeed demand—interpretation. Too often history is as definitive and dry as the worst textbook because it ignores the small pieces that, when assembled, explain a topic. Students came to understand that all big stories begin with small bits of evidence, which when strung together and interpreted, allow a scholar—or high school student—to tell a story accurately.

Asking good questions is essential to analyzing the past and to thinking critically. Primary documents, by their nature do not come with easy answers. Students learned how to ask good questions, and, in so doing, developed critical-thinking skills, which are so necessary for analyzing primary sources. Understanding what they know from the materials as well as what they do not know is important in all classes—not just history.

Technology provides an excellent way to access and use interesting information from the past. Students discovered a vast electronic library of fascinating stories and artifacts from the past. By using technology, they investigated topics holding both personal and academic interest without ever leaving their keyboards.

START SMALL TO THINK BIG

As with anything, you would be wise to start small with things you've already found successful. What types of primary document lessons or resources do you already use successfully? Can the key components transfer to this new medium? Too often we think moving on to something new means starting all over again. It need not be so. If you're successful with a lesson, it's probably because it employs solid pedagogy and captures student interest. Shifting it to use technology should allow you to transfer the elements that made it successful and to expand it using the new resources.

Don't jump in and change your program too extensively to use electronic resources until you've experimented with them yourself. Beginning to work with students before you are comfortable with electronic resources will overwhelm both you and your students. Try sampling sites and activities. See which ones work best for you and your teaching style. And, make sure the technological considerations are ones with which you are comfortable.

Once you have some experience, try to construct goals and a yearlong plan. I start the year with having students work on simple search-and-analysis skills at a single site and then work up to independent PowerPoint research projects turned in electronically. Think "baby steps" before long strides. In fact, one of the reasons I like using the American Memory website so much is that it makes this kind of progression fairly easy to plan. The resources there span most of American history so there is a wealth of material for almost all time periods. It is in diverse formats so you can expose students to everything from diaries to motion pictures, sheet music to recorded music. For the most part, once students have learned the way the collections are organized and searched, you do not have to teach basic access again with each new assignment. Now there are other great websites on many topics, but whenever you shift your students to a new site, they need some adjustment time to figure out how to navigate and use it. That is not usually the case if you construct different assignments for different eras using just one website —the American Memory collections from the Library of Congress.

When all is said and done, there are no good reasons for *not* using the primary sources now available online from the Library of Congress. Doing so may require some adjustments and some learning (for both teachers and students), but the rewards far outweigh the drawbacks.

The next chapter addresses professional development opportunities that you can do on your own, or workshops you can design for colleagues in your school or your district. So, what are you waiting for? Log on, see what's available. Explore new ways to make your own courses even more effective!

NOTES

1. "The Conservation Movement at the Crossroads: The Hetch Hetchy Controversy" is an online lesson created as a part of the American Memory Fellows Program, available from http://memory.loc.gov/ammem/ndlpedu/lessons/97/conser1/xroads.html.

2. The Gettysburg Address is found in the Library of Congress online exhibition, available from http://www.loc.gov/exhibits/gadd/.

3. This item can be found with the search words "wood shack" in the collection *Northern Great Plains, 1880–1920* [online], available from http://memory.loc.gov/ammem/award97/ndfahtml/ngphome.html.

4. These two items can be found with the search words "funeral" and "prairie wedding" in the collection *Northern Great Plains*. Use the Gallery View to identify the photographs quickly.

5. "The Great Depression in Your Classroom" is a lesson plan designed for the American Memory Fellows Institute [online], available from http://memory.loc.gov/ammem/ndlpedu/educators/workshop/depression/dover.html.

CHAPTER EIGHT

Professional Development: The Road Ahead

Many years ago, when I had considerably more energy, I was an adjunct instructor at Catholic University's School of Library and Information Science where I taught an evening course on online searching. In the early 1980s, online searching did not mean Web resources. It meant proprietary systems like Dialog, BRS, and Orbit—the last two having long since disappeared from the information landscape. For me, teaching this course *was* my own form of professional development. While I used these systems in my "day job," I knew a whole lot more *after* teaching these workshops than I ever thought I did going into the job. It was my way of staying current.

My goal was to stay one day ahead of the students—most of whom also had full-time jobs—and sometimes that was a tough thing to do. While teaching this class, the greatest compliment I ever received was when one of the students expressed her appreciation for my understanding of life "in the trenches." The common experience and the understanding we shared made it easier for me to be an effective mentor.

And, it will be the same for you. Once you have used the American Memory collections, you will be familiar with the search protocol and have ideas about integrating the materials into your curricula. You will become an effective role model, able to help others understand how to use these wonderful resources. Your enthusiasm will shine through, and your respect for your colleagues and the work they do will energize you to want to do more. It will become a team effort because you will learn as much as your colleagues do about using these resources in fresh, innovative ways.

In this chapter, I will point out some things unique to the American Memory collections that can make or break your first professional development workshop. I'll suggest the essential things to cover—just as the guidebooks do—that you can tailor to your available time and your "traveling" companions' interests. I'll also highlight some of the materials on the Learning Page that you can modify for your particular audience. Professional development can be a personal journey of discovery—both for the workshop leader and the participants—especially when you are dealing with primary source materials. Don't feel that you need to be an expert to do this. You have what it requires: knowledge of the collections and an understanding of life as a teacher—in the trenches.

If you are planning an American Memory workshop—or a series of workshops—an important concept to keep in mind is that professional development is an ongoing process. This is true of all forms of professional development, but it is particularly true when learning how to use primary sources. It takes time to digest a new teaching strategy and incorporate it into your daily life. The value of mutual mentoring and coaching cannot be overstated. As you work with other educators, you will find your own understanding expanding in ways you had not imagined, and you will slide back and forth between giving and receiving tips about using primary sources. While formal workshops can jump-start the process of discovery, it is when individuals use the materials to facilitate their own instructional goals that true learning takes place.

Technical Considerations for Using American Memory

Most textual collections do not require special viewers except to see graphics embedded in the page.

For audio collections, you should have RealPlayer.

Most photograph collections contain .jpg and .gif files, which can be viewed by any browser without additional software. A number of photographic collections, however, provide high-resolution .tif files that require a special viewer.

Map collections do not require special software for online viewing. If, however, you wish to use digital maps offline with all the zooming features of online access, you will want to download the MrSID viewer for local installation. That viewer is currently only available for a PC and requires 5MB of hard disk space.

Motion picture collections can be accessed with QuickTime or RealPlayer.

Some interactive Learning Page materials require Shockwave and Flash.

OPTIMAL EQUIPMENT AND INTERNET CONNECTIVITY

If technology is not your strongest suit, first identify what you *must* have and then figure out *who* can help you get there. Your knowledge of the American Memory collections and their potential use is far more important than your technology skills. You must have some, but you will find your comfort zone and operate within it. Or, you will find a colleague with whom to partner. Collaboration among colleagues builds tight bonds, and before you know it, you are adding to each other's professional growth. Don't be afraid to ask for help when you need it.

I'm reminded of a TV commercial featuring James Earl Jones that hyped a mobile telephone service by stating the obvious: "The call goes through." Likewise, when accessing digital information, the computer has to work. You will need a computer that is considered "multimedia" because the American Memory collections contain textual, audio, and video components. Typically these files are large, so for good performance, you will also need high-speed broadband Internet access—a cable modem, a DSL (digital subscriber line) or T-1 Internet connection. This is crucial. Without high-speed connectivity, much of the multimedia content will load very slowly. While more detail is provided later in this chapter, consult the sidebar "Technical Considerations for Using

American Memory" to get a bird's-eye view of basic technical considerations for optimal performance.

If you do not have optimal equipment, it does not mean that you cannot access the American Memory collections or the Learning Page. It does mean, however, that your experience—and your students' experiences—will be different. You will not have some of the interactive activities that today's students have come to expect, and the system response time may be slower than expected.

WORKSHOP MODELS: "STARTER" IDEAS

With the machines configured and wired properly, plug-ins and other software loaded, you're ready to go. This section suggests essential workshop topics, highlights Learning Page resources already developed for these purposes, and suggests successful orientation strategies. These models are just "starter" ideas, and they can be mixed and matched in any number of ways. Plus, you can revise and customize the handouts and other materials found on the Learning Page to meet your specific needs. I am hoping that some of these materials will jump-start your professional development journey so that you don't have to create your presentation or syllabus from scratch. Once started, you will discover many more ways to share your experience and knowledge. When you find something that works well, pass your comments along to the Learning Page reference librarian by following the "Questions?" link on the bottom right-hand corner of each Learning Page section. Refer to the chart below for professional development resources available on the Learning Page.

Learning Page Professional Development Materials

About Primary Sources

Getting Started: Primary Sources
http://memory.loc.gov/ammem/ndlpedu/start/p_src_1.html

Lesson Framework
http://memory.loc.gov/ammem/ndlpedu/lessons/fw.html

Using Primary Sources in the Classroom
http://memory.loc.gov/ammem/ndlpedu/lessons/primary.html

About Online Searching

Online Search Gallery
http://memory.loc.gov/ammem/ndlpedu/educators/workshop/search/gallery.html

Finding Items in American Memory
http://memory.loc.gov/ammem/ndlpedu/orientation/find.html

Synonym List
http://memory.loc.gov/ammem/ndlpedu/orientation/synonym.html

Choosing Search Words
http://memory.loc.gov/ammem/searchtp/amwords.html

What American Memory Resources Are Included in This Search?
http://memory.loc.gov/ammem/searchtp/amwords.html

Tips for New Users
http://memory.loc.gov/ammem/searchtp/amindex.html#simm

Bibliographic Record Search Options
http://lcweb2.loc.gov/ammem/searchtp/ambscrch.html

Full Text Search Options
http://memory.loc.gov/ammem/searchtp/amtsrch.html

(Cont'd)

Learning Page Professional Development Materials (Cont'd)

Document Analysis Worksheets

Photo-Analysis Sheet
   http://memory.loc.gov/ammem/ndlpedu/lessons/97/
   photo/analysis.html

What Do You See? Photo-Analysis Guide
   http://memory.loc.gov/ammem/ndlpedu/educators/
   workshop/discover/guide4.html

How Does It Read? Guide
   http://memory.loc.gov/ammem/ndlpedu/educators/
   workshop/discover/guide3.html

What Do You Hear? Guide
   http://memory.loc.gov/ammem/ndlpedu/educators/
   workshop/discover/guide2.html

Graphic Organizer: Thinking about Maps
   http://memory.loc.gov/ammem/ndlpedu/features/
   maps/organizer.pdf

Media Analysis Tools
   http://memory.loc.gov/ammem/ndlpedu/lessons/
   media.html

Handouts

American Memory Historical Collections: Catalog
   http://memory.loc.gov/ammem/ndlpedu/
   educators/handouts/am_coll.pdf

Exploring the Library of Congress via the Internet
   http://memory.loc.gov/ammem/ndlpedu/
   educators/handouts/handout2002.pdf

Why Use Primary Sources
   http://memory.loc.gov/ammem/ndlpedu/
   educators/handouts/prsrc.pdf

Toolkit for Finding Treasures in American Memory
   http://memory.loc.gov/ammem/ndlpedu/
   educators/handouts/toolkit2.pdf

Workshops and Materials

Discovering American Memory
   http://memory.loc.gov/ammem/ndlpedu/
   educators/workshop/discover/index.html

Historian's Sources
   http://memory.loc.gov/ammem/ndlpedu/lessons/
   psources/source.html

Prospecting in American Memory
   http://memory.loc.gov/ammem/ndlpedu/educators/
   workshop/prospecting/prover.html

Searching American Memory
   http://memory.loc.gov/ammem/ndlpedu/educators/
   workshop/search/index.html

*Creative Portraits: Using Art and Artifacts to Deepen
Historical Understanding*
   http://lcweb2.loc.gov/ammem/ndlpedu/educators/
   workshop/portraits/pover.html

*Emblematic Illustrations: Using Material Culture
to Interpret African American Life*
   http://lcweb2.loc.gov/ammem/ndlpedu/educators/
   workshop/emblematic/eover.html

Technical Information

Viewing and Listening to American Memory Collections
   http://memory.loc.gov/ammem/ndlpedu/resources/
   tech/amviewer.html

Linking and Bookmarking in American Memory
   http://memory.loc.gov/ammem/ndlpedu/resources/
   tech/link.html

Video Conferences

List of Programs
   http://memory.loc.gov/ammem/ndlpedu/educators/
   video/index.html

The Opening Show: 45 Minutes

To get your colleagues, principal, or parents fired up about the possibility of using primary sources in the classroom, you want a crisp, compelling presentation. The goal of an informational briefing like this is *to raise awareness* about primary sources and *to generate excitement* about how to get started using them at your school. Depending upon your audience and their interests, you may have more specific goals. If so, couch your presentation in a way that anticipates the questions you think they will ask. But, keep it simple—and short. Regardless of the "wrap" you put on your presentation, here are some basic questions that you can address in 45 minutes:

Why use primary sources with students?

What is American Memory?

What are primary sources?

Where do you find primary sources?

Why use primary sources with students? This is the nub of the matter, isn't it? Primary sources can awaken or renew students' interest in history because they provide fascinating stories and generate many questions about what happened and why. They make history "relevant." They sharpen critical-thinking and research skills, and they help students think like historians. The experience you have had with your students is the reason you are interested in passing this information on to other educators. Speak from your heart. If you can, start with an "aha" experience you have had with students that illustrates how primary sources spark the intellect.

For extra ammunition, go to the "Professional Development" section of the Learning Page, and look for the "Handouts" link. There you will find the document "Why Use Primary Sources with Students." This document is available both as a web page, which you can use as a visual for your talk, and as an Adobe PDF file, which you can also print as a handout. This two-page document discusses the instructional nature of primary sources and provides examples of student and teacher testimonies. You may be able to come back to this handout at the end of your presentation and tie the themes discussed in it to local or regional learning standards that you are obliged to address in your school.

What is American Memory? What are primary sources? Where do you start summarizing the gist of this massive website and its potential for education? Many teachers do not have the time to explore online, and others may be tentative about the technology. You, on the other hand, are so immersed in the American Memory collections and its primary sources that focusing on the essence—what you can pack into 45 minutes—may be difficult. You have so much to tell and so little time to tell it! Fortunately, introductory material already exists online, so much of this work is already done for you.

Begin by opening the Learning Page and go to the "Getting Started" section. There you will see a brief textual description of American Memory (see figure 8-1). You can use this web page almost as a "slide," a visual aid that can supplement your discussion of American Memory and the *free* primary-source materials it contains. You'll notice a "tell me more" link. This is the best part. Follow that link and you will have a ready-made interactive presentation defining primary sources and providing examples of primary sources from the American Memory collections.

Where do you find primary sources? Go to the Library of Congress website and click on American Memory. Now you are flying solo, so choose your examples carefully. Go next to Search across all collections. Pick a topic—and work this out ahead of time—that you have researched and that is relevant to a curriculum topic taught at your school; look for one that includes different media formats. Show the result of this search using the gallery view. For example, the automobile's impact on society was substantial in the 1920–1930 era, and a simple search on "automobile motor car" reveals photographs, sheet music, and films sure to fascinate today's students (see figure 3-7 on page 48).

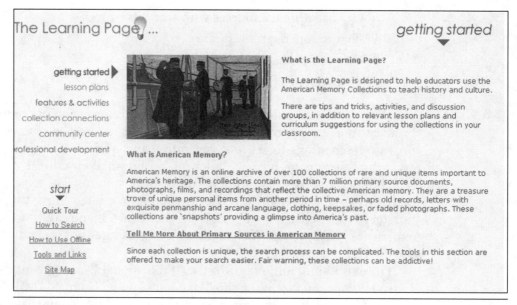

Figure 8-1
The Getting Started section of the Learning Page will help you understand primary sources and the best way to get started using them.

A bare-bones presentation like this should leave room for lots of questions. You will want to consider how you will handle them. Be prepared to respond to questions by showing materials from the Learning Page, such as student activities and teacher-prepared lessons. Generally, responding to a search question—"Find me something on World War II"—is the kind of thing that is risky in front of a group unless you are a search wiz and very familiar with the content of the collections in that area. Rather than execute a search, if you know of a relevant collection, it is sometimes better just to open the home page of that collection. In this case, showing the home pages of the *Hannah Arendt Papers* collection or the *Ansel Adams's Manzanar* collection might be all that's required. You can lose an audience like this very quickly if you get drawn into explaining the intricacies of search protocol.

The Introductory Workshop: Half Day or Full Day

An introductory in-service workshop should get into the nuts and bolts of using primary sources with students and provide workshop participants with hands-on exposure to the digital materials. The major emphasis should be on the materials—why and how to use them with students. Depending upon the audience, an in-service workshop should provide some initial background on searching, but keep it simple. Your basic goal should be for workshop participants to become familiar with the collections, excited about their use, comfortable enough with the technology to explore on their own, and eager to come back for more. You want to excite, but not overwhelm.

How to do this? Rule number one: make it relevant to the participants' needs. Ditch the educational theory and have fun. Rule number two: don't expect "to cover" American Memory in three hours. Generate enthusiasm and questions. Rule number three: level the playing field. Be prepared to learn as much as workshop participants do. Collaboration is the name of the game.

It is not possible to conduct an American Memory introductory workshop in less than three hours if you wish to make it interactive and personal. In fact, if you have the luxury of a full day with three-hour morning *and* afternoon sessions, that would be even better. There is so much to know and understand that developing a workshop usually works best if you think in a modular fashion. Consider what is basic for your participants and include that in the introductory workshop, however long you choose to make it. Then plan additional modules that can be offered at other times.

INTRODUCTORY WORKSHOP BASIC COMPONENTS

Here's where the Learning Page shines. By example, make sure workshop participants understand that the best way to explore the American Memory collections, at least in the beginning, is to start with the Learning Page. Begin with the Learning Page tutorial on American Memory and primary sources mentioned earlier in this chapter (see figure 8-1), but take it a little deeper: The four themes discussed in the informational briefing will come out in the discussion, but the basic components of a workshop should be more concrete: *finding primary sources, analyzing primary sources,* and *continuing the dialog.*

STEP 1: *Finding Primary Sources*

THE COLLECTION FINDER

Fundamental to understanding how to find material is intellectually grasping the scope of the primary-source collections—their depth and breadth. You can illustrate this by using the Collection Finder (see figure 3-1) to review the list of collections. Then, highlight specific collections that relate to your school's curricula requirements. Sometimes just showing the home pages of a few collections and a few selections from the collections will provide sufficient evidence of its usefulness. Or, you can refer to the American Memory collection catalog that is available on the Learning Page. Go to the "Professional Development" section and look for the "Handout" link. There you'll see an alphabetical list of titles and descriptions of all American Memory collections. You can view this as a web page or print it as a handout for reference.

Doing a cross-collection search on a topic of interest, as discussed earlier in this chapter, is also an excellent way to show scope and coverage as well as suggest some of the intricacies associated with searching. Unless you have a room full of library media specialists, you don't want to dwell too much on searching at this point. For those who "just can't wait," you could pass out the Library of Congress handout "Toolkit for Finding Treasures in American Memory" for independent use. This is available on the Learning Page, under Professional Development in the Handouts section.

THE ONLINE SEARCH GALLERY

As a way of introducing a little "discovery" and sharing into the search process, consider the search "Gallery," an exercise that was originally designed for a Library of Congress distance-learning course. While the course is no longer offered by the library, the materials are still available on the Learning Page. To find this exercise, go to the Learning Page, the Professional Development section, and choose the Self-Serve option. Scroll down the page until you come to the Search Skills section. There you will find the option "Searching American Memory." Click on that link and go to Course Activities. The first activity is the search gallery.

In this exercise designed by Judith Graves, workshop participants choose a favorite image from the search gallery and are then launched into that collection to explore independently. This exercise is great because it is personal and hands-on: it provides participants with an opportunity to introduce themselves to each other and gives each of them a glimpse of one American Memory collection.

The activity starts with a preselected item from a specific American Memory collection, which typically gets participants interested in the content and provides an incentive for learning more about that collection. After a time, participants report back to the group to introduce themselves and to share their quick impressions of the collection. They are encouraged to state why they picked the particular image that they did and to tell what they have learned about the collection during their brief independent online exploration. (Note: If you are clever designing web pages, you could take this activity and select other images that might be more relevant to your own teachers' curriculum interests.)

THE COLLECTION CONNECTIONS

Next, lead workshop participants to the collections through the "Collection Connections" section of the Learning Page. While this feature does not exist for every collection, where it does, you should encourage educators to consult it first—before beginning to search. Collection Connection documents provide historical context to the collection, simple search tips on curriculum topics, and teaching ideas that work with the materials in the collection.

If you have chosen to use the online search-gallery exercise, after the group discussion you might go to the Collection Connection section of the Learning Page and explore *Panoramic Maps, 1847–1929*. I chose this collection because one of the gallery items is a map, and the concept of using maps as teaching tools is new to many teachers. But, you could use any collection for which there is a Collection Connection. Demonstrate the interactivity between the Collection Connection and the online collection. Use some of the search examples provided; engage the group in discussion about the materials—how they might be used in a classroom situation.

THE FEATURES AND ACTIVITIES

It is always a little difficult to strike the right balance between teaching skills versus showing "neat stuff" when introducing these collections to educators. Typically, library media specialists will eventually want to get their hands dirty learning the intricacies of search protocol. Teachers could care less about the search details; they just want to find fantastic materials on *exactly* the topic they are teaching . . . *right now*!

To hook teachers, consider using the "Features and Activities" section on the Learning Page. Here you will find interactive presentations for teachers and activities for students that relate to themes typically studied in K–12 schools. Of particular importance is the American Memory Timeline (see figure 3-3) that provides access to the collections by topics and historical eras.

However you choose to introduce the concept of finding materials, remember that the goal at this point is to highlight the importance of knowing how to access an extensive archive—not to teach specific search techniques. If workshop participants are mostly teachers, this would also be a good time to talk about teaming up with your school librarian. If participants are mostly librarians, you might discuss coming back for an additional workshop focused exclusively on searching.

STEP 2: *Analyzing Primary Sources*

Once participants have a sense for what is involved in finding primary source materials, it is important to learn how to analyze primary sources. Unlike textbooks and other secondary sources that carry implied authority, primary sources carry personal, often fragmented messages. Unless primary sources are analyzed and integrated into a larger context, their usefulness is questionable. Unless they are examined using carefully developed analytical skills, primary sources simply become illustrative objects for student reports. "Document" analysis, thus, is the heart of the matter and where you should place significant emphasis in the introductory workshop.

Among the Learning Page materials that can help on this important issue is a lesson plan called "Historian's Sources" and a self-serve workshop with the title "Discovering American Memory." Both explore the nature of primary sources and provide frameworks for analysis. You will want to examine both carefully, picking individual activities that meet your needs. Each, if completed in its entirety, would take close to three hours.

HISTORIAN'S SOURCES

"Historian's Sources," discussed briefly in chapter 1, designed by James Giese, is an excellent overview of primary sources and what makes the historical record. Designed initially for high school students, this lesson could also be used for a teachers' professional development workshop. When teachers experience what their students will be experiencing, creative ideas will emerge. To use this student lesson as a professional development workshop, lead your workshop participants through the two student activities "Mindwalk" and the "Primary Source Set." The Mindwalk activity requires you to think about your activities over the previous twenty-four hours and consider what evidence of your life you may have left behind. Thus, it reinforces the notion that primary sources are created by individuals and carry personal, usually fragmented, stories. The Primary Source Set is a selection of photographs that depict slavery prior to the Civil War. Use the activities associated with these preselected images (or select others on another topic of interest) to illustrate how to evaluate primary sources. Supporting materials are provided online. Note that both of these exercises can be done equally well offline, if you prefer.

DISCOVERING AMERICAN MEMORY

"Discovering American Memory" is a stand-alone professional development workshop designed to re-create the student experience for teachers (see figure 8-2). It contains a series of short exercises some of which link to Historian's Sources, but presents them interactively. While portions of it relate to secondary school, many of its activities are better suited to elementary and middle school. Designed by Linda Joseph, a school librarian and American Memory Fellow, this workshop highlights different kinds of collections and encourages closer examination of the materials. Among its most useful activities are a series of three exercises that relate to visual, auditory, and textual resources: What Do You See? What Do You Hear? How Does It Read? Each activity provides examples from the American Memory collections and a document-analysis form to help guide the students' questions.

VIDEOCONFERENCE WITH THE LIBRARY OF CONGRESS

While not designed specifically for the K–12 audience, *Working with Primary Sources* is a two-hour videoconference that could be integrated into an introductory workshop. Similar to the two previously mentioned workshops, this video-

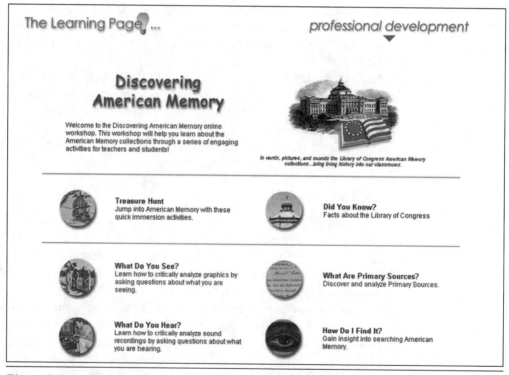

Figure 8-2
Discovering American Memory is a Library of Congress "self-serve" professional-development workshop designed to allow teachers to experience the collections as their students might.

conference addresses the nature of primary sources and how to evaluate them. Like other videoconferences from the Library of Congress, this requires a local facilitator and must be scheduled in advance. Reservations for this workshop can be made online via the Learning Page. Please note that you will need to contact the Library of Congress in sufficient time to schedule an equipment-compatibility check at least a week prior to the workshop. This and other distant-learning opportunities are available via an ISDN connection or Internet IP. Contact and technical information is available on the Learning Page in the Professional Development section.

STEP 3: *Continuing the Dialog*

Throughout this book, many references have been made to the Learning Page, but the "Community Center," brainchild of Leni Donlan, an American Memory Fellow and now Library of Congress staff, may deserve special attention. None of us can absorb tremendous amounts of material at one sitting, and most of us learn best in small doses. In the Community Center (see figure 8-3) you can "continue the dialog" with other teachers and with Library of Congress staff through regularly scheduled online discussions and chats, thus reinforcing the notion that professional development is a process, not an event. The Community Center discussions may highlight Learning Page features or American Memory collections not specifically addressed in your introductory workshop. You can also sign up for an

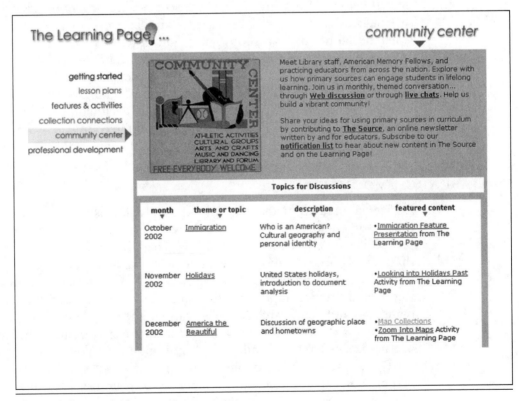

Figure 8-3
The Learning Page "Community Center" is a place for teachers and school library media specialists to exchange ideas about using primary sources.

online notification list that announces new materials available on the American Memory and Learning Page websites.

Desired Learning Outcomes

You want introductory workshop participants to leave with the sense that we all have much, much more to learn and experience and that there are many opportunities to do just that. They should not be overwhelmed, but empowered to try new things. You will want participants to understand that this exciting journey has just begun. You will want them to think about walking side by side with you down the road ahead. You will want them to understand that it will take time, but it will be a rewarding adventure.

Advanced Workshop Modules: 3 Hours

On the Learning Page, you will find more materials that will help you design additional modules to complement the basic half-day or full-day introductory workshop. Go to the "Professional Development" section of the Learning Page to see what is available. Most, but not all, of these self-serve workshops were originally developed for the American Memory Fellows Program discussed in chapter 2. All of these materials are suitable for you to use for your own professional development or to adapt for a workshop you may be designing for others. A few are highlighted below. Also available are videoconference programs provided by Library of Congress staff that can be used to supplement—or stand in lieu of—professional development workshops you might develop.

Three hours will probably be required for each new module you design. Most of these workshops will require a mix of presentation and hands-on exploratory time. All will require reflection and discussion. Planning for three hours makes them interchangeable, flexible, and easy to schedule. Each workshop essentially becomes a morning or afternoon event. They can be combined in lots of ways for maximum flexibility. Three models are suggested here, although many more are possible.

SEARCH MODULE

Designing a search module is, I think, essential. It is no secret that finding materials is sometimes difficult because there are differences, albeit small, in the search protocol from collection to collection. There are a variety of search techniques that, when known, can open up a new window on the American Memory collections. Each collection has "framing materials"—materials that describe the collection and provide important clues to effective searching in that collection. New materials (and new search features) can be added to existing collections. Things change. It is difficult to keep up in this dynamic environment. Because not everyone needs this level of detail, a workshop module makes sense.

Review the existing online searching materials on the Learning Page and perhaps you can find something adaptable for your use. These materials are accessible on the Learning Page in the "Professional Development" section under "self-serve." Warning: There have been significant systemwide improvements to the search protocol in recent years. Thus, many of the existing search workshop materials need revision. This is in no way a negative reflection on their creators, all of whom have moved on to other professional responsibilities. They are still available online simply because the structure and strategies employed continue to be sound.

Prospecting in American Memory

"Prospecting in American Memory" is a workshop developed for the American Memory Fellows Institute by Charlotte Bruce, a school librarian and American Memory Fellow. This workshop explores many of the techniques and strategies discussed in chapter 3. It explores how to expand the topic of "The West" through brainstorming language and provides search tips for the *California As I Saw It* collection, a bibliographic and full-text collection. The framework of this workshop is excellent. The search features of the collection *California As I Saw It* have been enhanced considerably since the workshop was designed, so revisions would be necessary before using it. However, the basic structure is helpful.

More Searching Workshops

"Searching American Memory" is an online course designed by Judith Graves at the Library of Congress and initially offered as a moderated course with a discussion module. While the library has not been able to continue this course, many of the materials—particularly the online search gallery discussed earlier—remain helpful and are still available online. Other activities and teaching techniques are useful as well.

A videoconference on searching the American Memory collections is another option for a follow-up search module that is currently available. This two-hour session is described in the "Professional Development" section of the Learning Page. "Treasure Hunting: Search Strategies for the American Memory Collections" is taught by Library of Congress digital reference staff. The handout developed for this offering is available on the Learning Page and, as discussed earlier in this chapter, could be used in other ways.

DOCUMENT-ANALYSIS MODULE

Beyond the basic introduction to primary sources, there is much to know about working with various primary-source materials and how to integrate analytical skills into the classroom experience. In the early years of the American Memory Fellows Program, the Library of Congress worked with Sonnet Takahisa, director of the New York City Museum School, and Gretchen Sorin, director of the Cooperstown Graduate Program of Museum Studies. They each developed a workshop: one on analyzing American Memory portraiture and the other on "material culture." Material culture is a term from the museum world that means man-made "stuff" that provides evidence of our lives. Examining material culture is much like Giese's "Mindwalk" activity discussed earlier in this chapter.

These workshops, originally developed and presented at the American Memory Fellows Institute, are now available on the Learning Page. They provide frameworks for teaching visual literacy and close observation of portraits and artifacts from the American Memory collections. Portions of these workshops could be effectively incorporated into a more advanced module on analyzing primary sources.

Visual Literacy through Creative Portraiture

"Creative Portraits: Using Art and Artifacts to Deepen Historical Understanding," developed by Takahisa, teaches object-observation skills, the most important of which is the ability to distinguish between subjective and objective observations. Students learn how museum curators assemble visual artifacts to tell a story. Working with a portrait of Billie Holiday from the *Creative Americans: Portraits from Carl Van Vechten, 1932–1964* collection, students make observations about the portraits distinguishing what they see in the portrait from what they know from prior experience. Visual clues to its historical meaning are discussed. This workshop could be modified by working with an image that is more directly related to a specific curriculum theme.

Visual Literacy through Material Culture

"Emblematic Illustrations: Using Material Culture to Interpret African American Life," developed by Sorin looks at a range of primary source materials—sheet music, photographs, first-person accounts, books, and broadsides—to learn about the popular culture from the Civil War time period to the early twentieth century. A significant emphasis is on how African Americans were portrayed and how they portrayed themselves during this period. To understand these reflections, the artifacts are considered within the larger historical framework of the time period. Students learn how "to read" an object and how to develop questions about the context in which it was developed. This is a powerful workshop. The materials chosen could be considered sensitive in some school districts and discussion about using difficult materials is a part of this workshop. Techniques used for examining material culture, however, could be used with many other topics and artifacts.

TECHNOLOGY MODULE

You may consider adding a couple of technology modules to your bag of professional development tricks. Inevitably, if participants are designing their own lesson plans, or even modifying existing ones, they will need to build web pages or PowerPoint presentations. There are some instructional materials and tips on the Learning Page, again in the "Professional Development" section, if you wish to go this route.

If you do go in this direction, the only thing that is unique to the American Memory collections is the manner in which you would link to an item in the collection.

Linking to American Memory Items

If you are intending to have workshop participants construct a lesson plan that requires linking to items within the American Memory collections, you will need to know something about American Memory web pages. While some web pages have "permanent" URLs, pages that appear as a response to your American Memory search are assembled "on the fly" and do not display a permanent URL. Rather they display dynamic URLs that are built as the search is executed. This means that the URL that appears on the top of your screen goes away after the search.

How, then, do you link to it from another web page or from a PowerPoint presentation? You must find the "permanent" URL in the source code. Instructions for doing this appear on the Learning Page in the "Getting Started" section. Find the page "Linking and Bookmarking in American Memory" for step-by-step guidance on how to do this.

IMPORTANT CONSIDERATIONS FOR TRAINING

Optimal Equipment

As noted earlier, because the American Memory collections provide so many types of historical artifacts, a robust computer system is required to access all components. If you have the newest and the greatest technology in your school, skip this section. But, if you are scouting out existing equipment that could be appropriated for workshop use, read on. Your workshop will be much easier, both for you and for the participants, with optimal equipment.

An optimal configuration would include a multimedia computer—a Pentium II 500 MHz running Windows 98 or higher or a Macintosh G3 300 MHz computer running OS 8.6 or higher. Each should be equipped with at least 256K memory and either Netscape 5.0 or Internet Explorer 5.0 or higher. The Internet browser must be properly configured with the correct plug-ins—multimedia viewers and players. On a PC, you will need to add QuickTime and either RealPlayer (now RealOne, available from realnetworks.com) or Windows Media Player to hear and view the audio and video components. On a Mac, because QuickTime is included in the operating system, you will only need to add RealPlayer. These applications can be downloaded for free. With the exception of .tif images, most computers will come equipped with both .jpeg and .gif viewers, which are normally acceptable for on-screen display of photographs.

The Learning Page provides more information in the "Getting Started" section about these issues. Because multimedia content is so engaging to today's students, you want to get this correct right from the start. Many of the Learning Page activities are interactive and require specialized software to experience their full functionality. Thus, you will want to add Shockwave and Flash if you don't already have it. Windows 98 and the Mac OS 8.6, the recommended system configurations, already incorporate Flash. Like the plug-ins required for the primary-source collections, Shockwave can also be downloaded for free. Those Learning Page applications that require Shockwave have a link to the download site. If you do not have optimal equipment, you will still be able to use the Learning Page materials, but those designed to be interactive will be static. Some of the handouts and other materials on the Learning Page are in Adobe Acrobat (pdf) format. Thus, you will also want to download the reader software, available for free from Adobe.

Filtering Software

If you have prepared your workshop at home, be sure to test it at school, if that is where your workshop will be given. While it sounds unbelievable, in at least one school system in this country, searches on the Library of Congress site were blocked because the filtering software used by that school system initially rejected websites with tildes in their URL. (Tildes are often used to flag personal websites.) In American Memory collections, the tilde appears in the temporary file name used in the dynamic displays—the page that is returned as a result of a search. If your school uses filtering software, because of sensitive topics represented in some of the collections, you may have other surprises. And, surprises like this are never good.

Space and Logistics

If you have opted for a formal, modular professional development program, you'll need to consider how your instructional goals relate to space and logistics. Will you be presenting an informational session or will you want your workshop participants to have hands-on practice? Consider, for example, if you only have forty-five minutes to show the district social studies coordinator and high school principals the American Memory collections. You'd probably opt for the lecture style, using a laptop and a projection unit. You'd make the session "interactive" by encouraging questions and participation. Your goal, in this case, might be to have them request a half-day, hands-on in-service for their social studies teachers. Happily, you'd only have to worry about your computer behaving properly.

If you were planning a session for teachers or librarians, however, hands-on activities are always best. This means you'll need a computer lab or an area where multiple computers can be clustered for the workshop. Do not assume anything. There is nothing worse than having the computers fizzle out in the middle of your workshop, so check out your equipment needs right from the start. Or better yet, if you have a technician who can help, include that person from the very beginning of your planning. In addition to the computers, check the printers to be sure that the drivers are properly installed. If you intend to schedule a videoconference with Library of Congress staff as a part of your workshop, a "preflight" equipment check will be required.

SUSTAINING PROFESSIONAL DEVELOPMENT

Most of us who love our professions get involved one way or the other with professional development. It could be through professional associations like the American Association of School Librarians and other such organizations, through graduate programs, through our own institutions. We help colleagues. We ask questions. We answer questions. We solve problems. We share resources. We swap ideas. We critique our work. We network. We write articles for professional journals. We write books. We present at conferences. We design workshops, websites, and learning activities. In short, we are involved beyond the standard work or school day in extending our own professional knowledge—in sustaining our own professional development.

Based on my experience, designing workshops on primary sources for your colleagues can become your own professional development as you learn more about primary sources and integrate them into your curriculum. Most of us learn best by doing, and particularly by doing something we need to do or need to know about. With humility and humor, make it fun, hands-on, practical, interactive, and participatory. Understand that the goal of any good coach is to pass "the torch" on to others in time. Pack these tips into your bag as you set off on the exciting road ahead. The experiences you encounter along the road ahead may just surprise you (see figure 8-4).

Figure 8-4
The road ahead with primary sources? Where will your professional journey take you? This 1937 photograph by Dorothea Lange appears in the American Memory collection, *America from the Great Depression to World War II: Black-and-White Photographs from the FSA-OWI, 1935–1945.*

CHAPTER NINE

Going to
the Source

I borrow a page from Jim Giese's foreword to this book in which he describes his style of teaching history as "going to the source." When teachers go to the source—when they access vast arrays of primary sources—they find many innovative ways to personalize history and hook their students on historical inquiry. When students are engaged in historical inquiry, they have a stake in their own learning. They display greater motivation to learn *and* to understand. Few could disagree that teaching for understanding is what education is all about. Many of the testimonies of the contributing authors in this book underscore this deceptively simple concept.

While the facts of history—who, what, where, and when—provide structure, it is the stories behind the facts that make them memorable and "real." All too often, teachers are required *to cover* the textbook that condenses eras into chapters and wars into paragraphs, leaving little time for historical inquiry *to uncover* issues, questions, and deeper meaning. While often required to use primary sources, few elementary and secondary teachers have had the time to learn the intricacies of using primary sources in instruction or figured out how to wedge them into the required curriculum. Analyzing primary sources requires that students consider different viewpoints, how they are expressed, and what they may represent. When students go to the source they must think. They must make informed judgments about events or topics—about what happened and why—to uncover the deeper meaning. They must consider "my" history and "your" history because "our" history as a nation is a composite of many stories. When students focus on the questions that emerge from these different perspectives, the picture becomes increasingly more intricate. As one middle school student put it, while it may look simple, "the thoughts in it run deep."

AN UNPARALLELED EDUCATIONAL RESOURCE

To many Americans "going to the source" means going to the Library of Congress, the nation's oldest federal cultural institution and the world's largest research library. If you were to sit in the Library of Congress's main reading room and gaze upward, you would see the beautiful domed ceiling shown in figure 9-1. Built in 1887, the Jefferson Building, which now houses this reading room, was restored to its original beauty and renovated almost one hundred years later with modern communications technology. Today, you can sit in the main reading room and plug in your laptop computer.

Likewise, access to the library's collections continues to expand. The digitization project that the Library of Congress began on a demonstration basis in the early 1990s has grown today into an unparalleled educational resource—the American Memory Historical Collections. The primary sources that are available in this digital collection now number over 7.5 million items, and this number will continue to grow in the years ahead. Never before has a digital archive of this size been assembled for *free* educational use.

As more and more educators become accustomed to finding teaching materials on the Web, the demand for these Library of Congress materials may skyrocket. Indeed, this was the finding of a proprietary survey done for the Library of Congress by Peter D. Hart Research Associates in 1999. Nine out of ten educators (89%) who completed this survey recognized that teachers will increasingly supplement traditional materials with web-based information. An equally high proportion of educators (87%) believed that it is appropriate to use primary-source materials within their disciplines and with their current students. These findings reveal a potentially huge audience for digital primary sources among educators with Web access. Given its mission and far-reaching constituencies, how can the Library of Congress make educators better informed about the availability of these materials?

Figure 9-1
This dome rising 160 feet above the Library of Congress's main reading room is awesome and inspiring.

The American Memory Fellows Program

The library initially addressed this question through the five-year (1997–2001) American Memory Fellows Program. Discussed in chapter 2, the Fellows Program was an innovative project for the Library of Congress and one that had as its goal to develop a small cadre of outstanding educators—leaders in their field—who would champion the use of Library of Congress primary resources in their schools and communities across the nation and help the library publicize its digital collections. A select group of 250 teachers and school media specialists have participated over the years, touching nearly every state in the nation, the District of Columbia, and the Virgin Islands. The "reach" of the American Memory Fellows, however, extends far beyond their small numbers.

Through the American Memory Fellows, the American Memory collections have become better known to hundreds, if not thousands, of K–12 educators. Their work is evident in the teacher-developed and -tested lesson plans now available on the Learning Page. The Learning Page itself has evolved under the leadership of American Memory Fellow Leni Donlan, (San Francisco). Also, Linda Joseph (Columbus, Ohio), Elizabeth Ridgway (Arlington, Va.), and Gail Petri (Rochester, N.Y.) have each contributed in significant ways to the professional development content on the Learning Page.

Other Fellows have replicated portions of the American Memory Fellows Program in local initiatives: Kathleen Ferenz launched a major two-year program modeled after the American Memory Fellows Program to introduce primary sources and the American Memory collections to hundreds of local teachers in the San Francisco Bay area. Agnes Dunn launched an educational institute in Fredericksburg, Virginia, modeled after the Fellows program designed to enhance public understanding of George Washington. Cynthia Stout received funds from the National Endowment for the Humanities (NEH) to plan and conduct a summer institute in Colorado highlighting primary sources. George Breaz implemented a districtwide distance-learning initiative in Nevada that has enabled the Library of Congress to test videoconferencing with teachers.

Still other fellows make the collections of the Library of Congress and their value to K–12 educators better known through their professional activities: As adjunct faculty in graduate-level courses, they include American Memory in their teacher and librarian curricula. Three of the contributing authors of this book are American Memory Fellows. Several fellows have published articles and other books, and many continue to be involved with primary-source workshops in their areas, with conferences, and with professional meetings. Many fellows "carry the torch" for Library of Congress and primary sources in more ways than we know.

Yet, this unparalleled resource is still unknown to many of the nearly three million elementary and secondary school educators in this country today. What else can the Library of Congress do to make the American Memory digital resources better known to other communities of learners?

The Adventure of the American Mind

The Adventure of the American Mind is a pilot project designed to introduce Library of Congress digital materials to teachers in western North Carolina where broadband Internet connectivity is not commonplace in schools. Initially designed to work with both pre-service and in-service teachers, this program sought to train two teachers from every school in the region on the library's resources and their application to K–12 education. Like the American Memory Fellows, each educator trained has a responsibility to train others in the use of the materials.

Under the leadership of the Education Research Consortium (ERC), an organization composed of representatives from local colleges and universities, Montreat College, Mars Hill College, and Brevard College in western North Carolina developed the program, designed the curriculum, and supported the first student cohort in 1999. Since then, the program has expanded with some modifications to Western Carolina University and Furman University in neighboring South Carolina, and most recently to home-school parents in western North Carolina, to Maricopa Community College in Arizona, to Southern Illinois University, and to public schools in Fairfax, Virginia. Since 1999, many hundreds of teachers and school library media specialists who otherwise may not have known of the American Memory collections have been trained on its use.

A CONTINUING JOURNEY

As you think about your professional goals, do they include learning more about primary sources? You may be a new teacher or an experienced one. You may be a library media specialist, a technology coordinator, or a school administrator. You may be good with technology or avoid it whenever you can. In your educational career, lots of "new" strategies for teaching and learning may have been introduced over the years, and perhaps you are weary of trying new things. Why should you get involved?

This concept—the concept of using primary sources—is not new, but the fact that these materials are so readily available is new. So, too, is the availability of the materials in digital format. Technology not only enables you to access these materials, it allows you to do things that are not possible with the actual artifact. For example, you can search through massive collections, you can quickly scan them visually, and you can zoom in on a particular feature of an old historical map or document. Through technology, you can do different things. And, you can do things differently.

As you look ahead, examine your own professional goals. Regardless of where you see yourself on the professional development curve, there are lots of opportunities to learn more about primary sources from the Library of Congress. As you explore the American Memory collections, you will find opportunities to grow professionally and bring new resources into your school community.

With significant professional development materials now available on the Learning Page, the Library of Congress is reaching out electronically to all teachers and school library media specialists interested in using digital primary sources with students. On all levels—from formal workshops provided at the Library of Congress for local educators to workshops delivered via videoconferencing, the Library of Congress continues to be interested in building a bigger and a more vibrant user community among K–12 teachers and media specialists.

If the American Memory collections truly are to become a catalyst to education and lifelong learning as envisioned by the Librarian of Congress, more and more educators must take ownership of their own professional development just as they urge their own students to do the same. Take advantage of the materials on the Learning Page. Check out the Community Center and join a chat or discussion group. Read the online newsletter *The Source*, available on the Learning Page for some getting-started ideas. Get a group of colleagues together and consider scheduling a videoconference with the Library of Congress. Use the materials in this book to teach yourself more about using primary sources.

As you make this professional journey, you may discover what many American Memory Fellows have testified: that the experience of using primary sources has changed the way they think about teaching and learning. You will find yourself immersed in interesting stories that illuminate our national history in a way that textbooks cannot. You will find yourself doing things differently: teaching through discovery and helping students form the questions that guide further study. You and your students will be uncovering our history and understanding more about our national past.

IMAGE CREDITS

In most cases, images are from the Library of Congress American Memory Historical Collections, the Library of Congress Online Exhibits, or the Library of Congress Learning Page at www.loc.gov. The title of the item, the Library of Congress Division that was responsible for digitization, and the reproduction number or digital identification (id) are provided, when available. When the title of a Library of Congress image has been supplied by the cataloger, the title appears in square brackets. Six images from research institutions that collaborated with the Library of Congress are included, and these images can also be searched within the American Memory website.

CHAPTER 1

1-1 Jefferson's "original Rough draught" of the Declaration of Independence, p.1. Library of Congress Manuscript Division: Jefferson Papers. Exhibits Online: *American Treasures of the Library of Congress:* http://www.loc.gov/exhibits/treasures/images/decp1.jpg

1-2 and 1-3 John Quinn. Library of Congress Prints and Photographs Division: Baseball cards from the Benjamin K. Edwards Collection. *Baseball Cards, 1887–1914.* Digital id: bbc 1507.

1-4 [Incidents of the war. A harvest of death, Gettysburg, July, 1863]. Library of Congress Prints and Photographs Division. *Selected Civil War Photographs, 1861–1865.* Reproduction number: LC-B8184-7964-A DLC; Digital id: ppmsc 00168.

CHAPTER 2

2-1 The *Library of Congress* website: http://www.loc.gov

2-2 The *American Memory Historical Collections:* http://www.memory.loc

2-3 *The Alexander Graham Bell Family Papers:* http://memory.loc.gov/ammem/bellhtml/bellhome.html

2-4 *The Hannah Arendt Papers:* http://memory.loc.gov/ammem/arendthtml/arendthome.html

2-5 *The African-American Experience in Ohio,* a joint project with the Library of Congress and the Ohio Historical Society: http://memory.loc.gov/ammem/award97/ohshtml/aaeohome.html

2-6   *By Popular Demand: Portraits of the Presidents and First Ladies:* http:// memory.loc.gov/ammem/odmdhtml/preshome.html

2-7   What Do You See? Photoanalysis Guide. The Library of Congress Learning Page: http://memory.loc.gov/ammem/ndlpedu/educators/workshop/discover/guide4.html

2-8   Chilkat children on river bank, Klukwan, Alaska, 1894. University of Washington Libraries. Manuscripts, Special Collections, University Archives: John Francis Pratt Collection no. 567. *American Indians of the Pacific Northwest.* Negative number: NA3086.

2-9   "Autumn," poem by Helen Keller, 27 October 1893. The Library of Congress Manuscript Division: Alexander Graham Bell Family Papers. *Words and Deeds in American History.*

2-10   Letter, Mary Todd Lincoln to Abraham Lincoln advising her husband to remove the hesitant Gen. George B. McClellan from command, 2 November [1862]. Library of Congress Manuscript Division. *Words and Deeds in American History.* Reproduction number: A107 (color slide; p. 1 and 2).

2-11   The city of Boston. New York, Currier & Ives, 1873. Library of Congress Geography and Map Division. *Panoramic Maps, 1847–1929.* Digital id: http:// hdl.loc.gov/loc.gmd/g3764b.pm002750

2-12   Emigrants [i.e., immigrants] landing at Ellis Island/Thomas A. Edison, Inc. Library of Congress Motion Picture, Broadcasting, and Recorded Sound Division. *Life of a City: Early Films of New York, 1898–1906.* Digital id: http://hdl.loc. gov/loc.mbrsmi/lcmp002.m2a10987

2-13   The Online Exhibitions: http://www.loc.gov/exhibits

2-14   Today in History: http://memory.loc.gov/ammem/today/today.html

2-15   America's Library: http://www.americaslibrary.gov

CHAPTER 3

3-1   American Memory Collection Finder: http://memory.loc.gov/ammem/ collections/finder.html

3-2   The Library of Congress Learning Page: http://memory.loc.gov/ammem/ ndlpedu/index.html

3-3   American Memory Timeline: http://memory.loc.gov/ammem/ndlpedu/ features/timeline/index.html

3-4   Learning Page Collection Connection: Walt Whitman Notebooks: http://memory. loc.gov/ammem/ndlpedu/collections/ww

3-5   Learning Page Online Lesson: Grapes of Wrath: Scrapbooks and Artifacts: http:// memory.loc.gov/ammem/ndlpedu/lessons/01/grapes/index.html

3-6   American Memory All Collections Search Page: http://memory.loc.gov/ ammem/mdbquery.html

3-7   "Gallery" Display of American Memory Search Results

3-8   *Born in Slavery* Full-Text Search Page: http://memory.loc.gov/ammem/ mesnquery.html

CHAPTER 4

4-1   The Star Spangled Banner. Library of Congress Music Division. Exhibits Online: *American Treasures of the Library of Congress:* http://www.loc.gov/exhibits/ treasures/images/vc29.1.jpg

4-3 [Fair Oaks, Va. Lt. James B. Washington, a Confederate prisoner, with Capt. George A. Custer of the 5th Cavalry, U.S.A.] Library of Congress Prints and Photographs Division. *Selected Civil War Photographs, 1861–1865.* Digital id: http://memory.loc.gov/service/pnp/cwpb/00100/00156t.gif

4-4 Yanke Doodle. Library of Congress Rare Book and Special Collections Division: Hand-colored Song Sheets collection. *America Singing: Nineteenth-Century Song Sheets.* Digital id: hc00037b.

4-5 Heroes of the Colored Race. Philadelphia 1881. Library of Congress Prints and Photographs Division. *African American Odyssey.* Reproduction number: LC-USZC2-10180 (5-7); Digital id: http://lcweb.loc.gov/exhibits/odyssey/archive/05/0507001r.jpg.

CHAPTER 5

5-1 [Gettysburg, Pa. Alfred R. Waud, artist of *Harper's Weekly,* sketching on battle-field]. Library of Congress Prints and Photographs Division. *Selected Civil War Photographs, 1861–1865.* Reproduction number: LC-DIG-cwpb-00074 DLC; Digital id: hdl.loc.gov/loc.pnp/cwpb.00074

5-2 [Suffrage parade, New York City, May 6, 1912] Library of Congress Prints and Photographs Division. *By Popular Demand: Votes for Woman Suffrage Pictures, 1850–1920.* Reproduction number: LC-USZ62-10845 DLC; Digital id: cph 3a52079.

5-3 Photo provided by Gail Petri.

5-4 Immigrants on an Atlantic liner. P&P Online Catalog. Reproduction number: LC-USZ62-10845 DLC; Digital id: cph 3a52079.

5-5 S. D. Butcher photographing babies at Broken Bow, Nebraska. Nebraska State Historical Society: Butcher, Solomon D. (Solomon Devore), 1856–1927. *Prairie Settlement: Nebraska Photos and Family Letters, 1862–1912.* Reproduction number: RG2608.PH:000000-002943; Digital id: nbhips 13268.

5-6 Receipt for African-American slave. The Filson Historical Society: Corlis-Respess Family Papers. *First American West: The Ohio River Valley, 1750–1820.*

CHAPTER 6

6-1 No enemy sub will dare lift its eye if you lend your Zeiss or Bausch & Lomb binoculars to the Navy: pack carefully, include your name and address : send to Naval Observatory Washington D.C. Library of Congress Prints and Photographs Division: Work Projects Administration Poster Collection. *By the People, For the People: Posters from the WPA, 1936–1943.* Reproduction number: LC-USZ62-59982; Digital id: http://hdl.loc.gov/loc.pnp/cph.3b07722.

6-2 Rural school. This school had five cases of scabies out of the fifteen attending. Williams County, North Dakota. Library of Congress Prints and Photographs Division: Farm Security Administration — Office of War Information Photograph Collection. *America from the Great Depression to World War II: Black-and-White Photographs from the FSA-OWI, 1935–1945.* Reproduction number: LC-USF34-030798-D DLC; Digital id: fsa 8b20035.

6-3 [Zora Neale Hurston. Eatonville, Florida, 1935]. Library of Congress American Folklife Center. *African-American Odyssey.* Digital id: http://lcweb2.loc.gov/ammem/aaohtml/exhibit/aopart7b.html#0712.

CHAPTER 7

7-1 Home is where the heart is. North Dakota State University Institute for Regional Studies: Fred Hultstrand History in Pictures Collection, NDIRS-NDSU, Fargo. *Northern Great Plains 1880–1920.* Digital id: ndfahult b275.

7-2 A funeral in pioneer days. North Dakota State University Institute for Regional Studies: Fred Hultstrand History in Pictures Collection, NDIRS-NDSU, Fargo. *Northern Great Plains 1880–1920.* Digital id: ndfahult b234.

7-3 Ole Myrvik wedding, Milton, North Dakota, 1894. North Dakota State University Institute for Regional Studies: Fred Hultstrand History in Pictures Collection, NDIRS-NDSU, Fargo. *Northern Great Plains 1880–1920.* Digital id: ndfahult b437.

7-4 An abandoned farm. Cimarron County, Oklahoma. Library of Congress Prints and Photographs Division: Farm Security Administration—Office of War Information Photograph Collection. *America from the Great Depression to World War II: Black-and-White Photographs from the FSA-OWI, 1935–1945.* Reproduction number: LC-USZ62-131310 DLC; Digital id: fsa 8b38302.

7-5 Oklahoma drought refugees stalled on highway near Lordsburg, New Mexico. Library of Congress Prints and Photographs Division: Farm Security Administration—Office of War Information Photograph Collection. *America from the Great Depression to World War II: Black-and-White Photographs from the FSA-OWI, 1935–1945.* Reproduction number: LC-USF34-016681-C DLC; Digital id: fsa 8b38635.

CHAPTER 8

8-1 The Library of Congress Learning Page, Getting Started: http://memory.loc.gov/ammem/ndlpedu/start/index.html

8-2 Discovering American Memory workshop: http://memory.loc.gov/ammem/ndlpedu/educators/workshop/discover/index.html

8-3 The Library of Congress Learning Page, Community Center: http://memory.loc.gov/ammem/ndlpedu/community/index.html

8-4 Towards Los Angeles. Library of Congress Prints and Photographs Division: Farm Security Administration—Office of War Information Photograph Collection. *America from the Great Depression to World War II: Black-and-White Photographs from the FSA-OWI, 1935–1945.* Reproduction number: LC-USZ62-55378 DLC; Digital id: cph 3b03265.

CHAPTER 9

9-1 Main Reading Room, domed ceiling. The Thomas Jefferson Building: A Virtual Tour of the Library of Congress, Second Floor. http://www.loc.gov/jefftour/images/dome-large.jpg

INDEX

SUSAN VECCIA, formerly manager of educational outreach for the Library of Congress, is now an independent library and education consultant. She managed the first large-scale program designed to make the Library of Congress's digital primary-source materials more accessible to K–12 teachers and school librarians. Concurrent with her work at the library, Susan was the founding editor of *Multi-Media Schools,* a subscription-based national magazine that addresses the practical concerns of teachers and librarians working with new technologies. Focusing on training and technical writing, she has worked in both public and school libraries. Throughout her career, she has served in various adjunct and advisory capacities including teaching at Catholic University School of Library and Information Science. She has an undergraduate degree from Connecticut College and a master's degree in library science from Catholic University.